View-Based 3-D Object Retrieval

Yue Gao
Qionghai Dai

Amsterdam • Boston • Heidelberg • London • New York • Oxford
ELSEVIER Paris • San Diego • San Francisco • Singapore • Sydney • Tokyo

Executive Editor: Steve Elliot
Editorial Project Manager: Lindsay Lawrence
Project Manager: Anusha Sambamoorthy
Designer: Matthew Limbert

Elsevier
Radarweg 29, PO Box 211, 1000 AE Amsterdam, Netherlands
225 Wyman Street, Waltham, MA 02451, USA
The Boulevard, Langford Lane, Kidlington, Oxford OX5 1GB, UK

Notices
Knowledge and best practice in this field are constantly changing. As new research and experience broaden our understanding, changes in research methods, professional practices, or medical treatment may become necessary.

Practitioners and researchers must always rely on their own experience and knowledge in evaluating and using any information, methods, compounds, or experiments described herein. In using such information or methods they should be mindful of their own safety and the safety of others, including parties for whom they have a professional responsibility.

To the fullest extent of the law, neither the Publisher nor the authors, contributors, or editors, assume any liability for any injury and/or damage to persons or property as a matter of products liability, negligence or otherwise, or from any use or operation of any methods, products, instructions, or ideas contained in the material herein.

Library of Congress Cataloging-in-Publication Data
A catalog record for this book is available from the Library of Congress

British Library Cataloguing in Publication Data
A catalogue record for this book is available from the British Library

ISBN: 978-0-12-802419-5

For information on all Elsevier publications
visit our web site at store.elsevier.com

This book has been manufactured using Print On Demand technology. Each copy is produced to order and is limited to black ink. The online version of this book will show color figures where appropriate.

Working together
to grow libraries in
developing countries

www.elsevier.com • www.bookaid.org

View-Based 3-D Object Retrieval

CONTENTS

ACKNOWLEDGMENTS

Our thanks to Steve Elliot and Lindsay Lawrence from Elsevier, for their support on this book. We are grateful for their support in helping us develop a quality book.

We would also like to acknowledge the support of our institution, Tsinghua University, and the funding provided by NSFC for the project of view-based 3-D object retrieval.

Thanks to our colleagues from the Department of Automation and members of the Broadband Network and Digital Multimedia Lab at Tsinghua University. Special thanks to Dr Fei Li, for his technical expertise, enthusiasm, and willingness to always help. Also special thanks to Dr Weizhi Nie, for patiently reviewing earlier versions of portions of this manuscript and the high-quality comments and suggestions that improved this book significantly.

Finally, and most importantly, a very heartfelt thank you to our families, for their constant support, encouragement, patience, and understanding during the whole journey.

PREFACE

Content-based 3-D object retrieval has attracted extensive research attention and has applications in a variety of fields, including computer-aided design, telemedicine, mobile multimedia, virtual reality, and entertainment. The requirements for an efficient and effective content-based 3-D object retrieval technique have increased tremendously to enable fast 3-D reconstruction and model design. Recent technical progress, such as the development of camera technologies, has made it possible to capture the views of 3-D objects. As a result, view-based 3-D object retrieval has become an essential but challenging research topic.

We initiated our work on view-based 3-D object retrieval in 2006: this project was supported by the National Natural Science Foundation of China and Tsinghua University. Our objective was to design and implement methods and systems that were capable of indexing and retrieving large-scale 3-D objects based on content information. During the course of this project, we focused on key challenges in view-based 3-D object retrieval and proposed several methods and solutions in this field.

The objectives of this book are to introduce the fundamental problems, to review a collection of selected and state-of-the-art methods, and to introduce our work in this emerging and developing research field. We furthermore summarize recent achievements in 3-D object retrieval.

Generally, there are four main challenges in view-based 3-D object retrieval: view extraction, view selection, view representation, and multiple-view comparison. We have designed a content-based 3-D object retrieval system targeting all these challenges. A spatial structure circular descriptor was introduced to extract the views generated from 3-D objects. To select discriminative views, we proposed the first interactive view selection framework, which could incrementally select representative views from a large pool of views with user relevance feedback. To learn the optimal weights for multiple views, our system employed a k-partite graph reinforcement learning process to automatically generate the weights for representative views.

We proposed several object matching methods for 3-D object retrieval, including bipartite graph matching and Gaussian Mixture Model formulation. To explore the structure underlying the labeled and unlabeled 3-D objects, we proposed to investigate learning-based methods on 3-D object retrieval. We proposed to learn the optimal Hausdorff distance metric for pairwise object matching to jointly learn the object relevance and bipartite graph matching metric in a graph structure, and to learn the object relevance in a hypergraph framework, which could handle the high-order information derived from multiple views.

Although there has been significant progress made in view-based 3-D object retrieval, challenges are still present and new opportunities present themselves rapidly. We discuss here these future studies, such as the issues of big data, feature extraction, multiple-view matching, multimodal data problem, and geolocation-based applications.

Beijing,   **Yue Gao**
October 2014   **Qionghai Dai**

PART I

The Start

This part, which serves as the introduction of the book, contains the first two chapters. In Chapter 1, the basic ideas and the background of 3-D object retrieval (3DOR) are introduced, including the comparison between model-based 3DOR (M3DOR) and view-based 3DOR (V3DOR), the main challenges of V3DOR, our contributions, and the structure of this book. In Chapter 2, we introduce the benchmark for 3DOR in recent years and the Shape Retrieval Contest (SHREC).

Introduction

1.1 THE DEFINITION OF 3DOR

Rapid advances in computer techniques and networks have led to large-scale multimedia data, which necessitate effective and efficient information retrieval. In the past several decades, multimedia information retrieval has been investigated extensively [1–3]. In recent years, computing graphics hardware and image processing techniques have made remarkable progress and 3-D technologies have been shown to be superior in various application fields, such as computer-aided design (CAD), medicine, virtual reality, and entertainment. For example, 3-D movies have become much more popular nowadays and their market is still increasing.

Traditional devices for collecting visual information, such as cameras and video recorders, are primarily used for 2-D information. Although 2-D information processing has been investigated for decades, 3-D data are superior for representing and processing stereo information.

The applications of 3-D technology can be traced back to the nineteenth century. In 1839, the English scientist Sir Charles Wheatstone invented the first stereoscope. Stereopsis is described by binocular vision, which was used to construct the stereoscope. Sir Charles Wheatstone explained that the impression of solidity was achieved by the combination of two individual views of the same objects, and these views were taken by our two eyes. Dr Patrick J. Hanratty, the father of computer-aided manufacturing (CAM), developed the first CAD software system in 1957, a numerical control programming tool that was also the first commercial CAM software. During that time, CAD modeling was still based on 2-D drafting. In 1965, a team led by Charles Lang from Cambridge University started conducting 3-D CAD modeling research. As a result, 3-D modeling became popular and has since been applied to various design tasks. In terms of entertainment, the first 3-D game "Night Driver" was released in 1976 by Atari. Nowadays, 3-D effects have become a central component of electronic games such as "World of War."

3

With the wide applications of 3-D technology, 3-D data provide quick increases in both local data storage and online data storage from the Internet. The growing stores of data naturally increase the urgent need for effective and efficient 3DOR methods. Although 3-D modeling has been investigated for decades, it is still a high-cost and laborious task to model highly realistic 3-D models. According to a report from Gunn [4], only 20% of designs should be started from the very beginning in industrial design, while 40% of designs can be achieved by combining existing designs, and the remaining 40% of designs can be obtained by just revising existing designs. This percentage breakdown indicates that the reuse and revision of existing 3-D models can significantly improve model design performance, which necessitates the importance of 3-D object search in industry.

The main task of 3DOR can be defined as follows [5]:

Given a query object, define appropriate measures to automatically assess the similarity between any pair of 3-D objects based on a suitable notion of similarity.

Considering the requirements of 3DOR, the "content-based" method is the preferred technique: this method has been shown to be superior in multimedia information retrieval. In comparison with existing 1-D and 2-D multimedia information retrieval techniques, 3DOR is still in its infancy. Traditional text-based 3DOR methods which suffer from low efficiency and accuracy, cannot be effectively employed. One important issue is that 3-D objects contain both shape and appearance information, which is beyond the scope of text-based representation. Under these circumstances, extensive research efforts [6–8] have been dedicated to 3DOR, in which the content-based information has been exploited for intrinsic feature representation and object matching.

1.2 MODEL-BASED 3DOR VERSUS VIEW-BASED 3DOR

Existing 3DOR methods can be generally categorized into two types: M3DOR and V3DOR. These categories differ in the data types that they employ and their corresponding methods. Most early methods belong to M3DOR, which explicitly requires existing virtual 3-D model information, such as point cloud data. In M3DOR, 3-D features are directly extracted from the virtual 3-D model. Typical features include low-level features such as surface distributions [9], geometric moments [10], surface geometries [11–15], volumetric descriptors [16, 17], and high-level features, such as skeleton-based descriptors [18]. In these feature extraction methods, 3-D object rotation, translation, and scaling should be taken into consideration. The advantage of M3DOR is that all the model information can be employed for processing, which is also a major limitation of M3DOR. In the case where no 3-D model is available, a 3-D model construction procedure is required to generate the virtual model via a collection of images. We note that 3-D model reconstruction is computationally expensive and that its performance is highly restricted to sampled images, which severely limits practical applications of M3DOR methods because 3-D model information is not available in many cases.

The other 3DOR method is based on views, in which each 3-D object is represented by a group of multiple views and the feature is extracted from these views. Compared with M3DOR, V3DOR is much more flexible because virtual 3-D model information is not mandatory. Another merit of V3DOR is that it benefits from existing image processing technologies [1, 19, 20], which have been extensively explored for many decades. As introduced in Daras and Axenopoulos [21], "view-based methods have the advantages of being highly discriminative, can work for articulated objects, can be effective for partial matching and can also be beneficial for 2-D sketch-based and 2-D image-based queries." V3DOR has been shown to be superior in 3-D object representation, in which only one or a few views are needed. Experimental results reported in Bustos et al. [22] and Shilane et al. [23] also demonstrated that V3DOR methods can achieve better performance than M3DOR methods.

1.3 THE CHALLENGES OF V3DOR

The general process of V3DOR is composed of four stages: view capture, view selection, feature extraction, and object matching, as shown in Figure 1.1.

Following the above procedure, the main challenges in V3DOR are fourfold.

- **Capturing views**

  In V3DOR, the obtained views are the fundamental elements for any analysis. Therefore, a set of optimally captured views can describe the 3-D objects well and further lead to better 3DOR performance. Existing methods usually build a predefined camera array, consisting of multiple cameras from determined directions, to capture views. It is noted that this is a high constrict considering the real-world applications, in which case it may be not feasible to capture the views from the predefined directions.

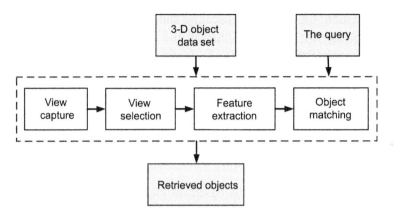

Figure 1.1 The general framework of V3DOR.

- **Selection of representative views**
  Generally, a large number of views not only provide rich information of 3-D objects, but also supply redundant data, which increase both the computational cost and difficulties in object matching. Selecting a set of representative views is an important but challenging task for 3-D object description.
- **Feature extraction**
  Although image processing has been investigated for many decades, extracting features for 3-D objects is different from extracting features for a single 2-D image. Unlike the single-image data used in general image retrieval tasks, the multiple views of 3-D objects are highly correlated. Therefore, the feature extraction should be able to explore the spatial correlation among these views.
- **Multiple-view-based object matching**
  In V3DOR, the multiple-view matching plays an important role in the final retrieval process. Multiple-view matching is significantly different from traditional one-to-one image matching. Considering the complex information associated with these multiple views, investigating the many-to-many view matching and estimating the relevance among 3-D objects are challenging tasks in V3DOR.

1.4 SUMMARY OF OUR WORK

We have exerted significant effort addressing these challenging tasks. In the past decade, we have made some advances and progress in research pertaining to V3DOR. In this book, we will discuss our recent progress in the content-based V3DOR systems, considering the four challenging aspects discussed above. Here, we briefly summarize our work.

1.4.1 View Extraction

View extraction is a fundamental and essential task in V3DOR. The images that are captured will be further employed for feature extraction and comparison. Extracting a group of adequate but compact views is a difficult problem in V3DOR. A well-selected group of multiple views should not only describe the 3-D object information from different directions, but also reflect the spatial structure of the 3-D object. Existing view-capture methods primarily extract a group of views using a predefined camera array. With the goal of developing a compact and flexible description method, we proposed a spatial-structure circular descriptor (SSCD) [24] to capture 3-D object information from the model. The basic idea behind SSCD is to obtain global information from 2-D images, preserving the spatial relationship. To generate the SSCD, a minimal bounding sphere of the 3-D model is constructed and the sampled points on the model surface are projected onto the bounding sphere. To further facilitate the representation of the global structure the bounding sphere is projected onto a plane, and the projection is a circle. SSCD can preserve the global spatial structure of the 3-D model information and is invariant to object rotation and scaling. To compare two SSCDs, the histogram information is extracted as the SSCD feature and two SSCDs from two compared 3-D objects are formulated in a bipartite graph structure. The optimal matching in the object bipartite graph is calculated by minimizing the matching distance between the two objects.

1.4.2 Representative View Selection

In most cases, V3DOR methods work on a group of pre-generated images. Besides the rich information provided by multiple views, having too many images also results in redundant information, which not only leads to high computational costs but may also degrade 3DOR performance if mismatching between multiple views occurs. Under these circumstances, representative view selection can be regarded as a preprocessing step for V3DOR. Representative view selection can be divided into two paradigms: a predefined camera array and view selection from the pool of views. For the first paradigm, the view selection procedure is conducted in the camera array setting for multiple-view capture. For the second paradigm, assuming that a group of views have been obtained (the pool of multiple views), our objective is to select a few views to represent the 3-D object. In the field of view selection from the pool, we proposed an interactive query view selection (QVS) method [25] to select representative views. In this method, a group of views are provided to describe the query object. View clustering is first conducted to group these views into clusters and one view is selected from each cluster to generate the pool of all query views. This step can reduce the initial redundancy of the query object. Next, one initial query view is selected from the pool of query views used for 3DOR. The top results are shown to the users and these results can be labeled with the user relevance feedback information. New queries can be selected from the pool of query views, which can better reflect the user's opinion of the results. A new distance metric can be determined based on what was learned from each newly selected query view. All the selected query views are combined using the learned weights for each next-round search. We iterate this process until We achieve satisfactory results. In summary, QVS is an incremental view selection method that takes user relevance feedback into consideration. This technique is different from existing representative view selection methods, which mainly select views in the view capture step. QVS can accordingly be a more discriminatory and efficient technique for representative view selection.

1.4.3 Learning the Weights for Multiple Views

In 3-D object representation, the descriptive capabilities of different views vary significantly. Some views may be able to very accurately describe 3-D objects, while other views may reflect very little information about the relevant object. Therefore, even with the selected representative views of the 3-D object, the optimal weights for these views are still essential to further improve the discriminatory power of these views. We proposed a k-partite graph reinforcement model to address this task [26]. The k-partite graph reinforcement model aims to determine the optimal weight for each vertex by considering the overall structure of the k-partite graph. In each round of 3DOR, the top search results are regarded as pseudo-relevant samples. These pseudo-relevant samples and the query object are formulated in a k-partite graph, in which multiple views of each object generate one partite of the graph. The k-partite graph reinforcement is conducted and the weights of these vertices are updated according to an iterative process. In this way, the views that are more informative and closer to pseudo-relevant objects can be assigned higher weights. This method can enhance the discriminatory properties of selected representative views.

1.4.4 Distance Measures for Object Matching

With multiple views of each 3-D object, the distance measure is the key piece of information for 3DOR, as discussed above. In light of the multiple views, the distance measure for 3-D objects can be regarded as a many-to-many matching scheme. There are several well-known distance measures, such as the Euclidean distance, the Minkowski distance, and the Mahalanobis distance. These conventional distance measures typically adopt simple principles to integrate the distances of view pairs between two compared objects. However, these methods may perform poorly in V3DOR because they can neglect the structure information of the multiple views for each 3-D object.

We accordingly proposed several 3-D object distance measures considering different circumstances. We briefly introduce these measures below.

- **Bipartite graph matching and learning**
  We proposed to employ bipartite graphs to formulate the relationship between two groups of views from two 3-D objects [27]. The representative views are first generated from each object and all representative views from one object are denoted by one part of the bipartite graph. The visual similarity between each of the two views from different objects generates one edge, which links the two vertices in the bipartite graph. Then, proportional max-weighted bipartite matching is conducted to measure the similarity between the two objects.

- **Probabilistic measure**
  To consider both the relevant and the irrelevant relationships between two objects, we proposed a probabilistic measure in [28]. In this method, the views of the query object are first grouped into view clusters. The selected representative views are employed to build the query model. To ensure an accurate 3-D object comparison, given a query object Q, a positive matching model $p(O|Q, \Delta = 1)$, and a negative matching model $p(O|Q, \Delta = 0)$ are trained using positive and negative matched samples, which are preselected from pairwise views. $p(O|Q, \Delta = 1)$ indicates the probability of one object O, given the query object Q when O is relevant to Q. $p(O|Q, \Delta = 0)$ indicates the probability of one object O given the query object Q when O is irrelevant to Q. The positive matching model and the negative matching model are used to estimate the probabilities that these two views are either matched or not. These probabilities are then combined to generate the final result, according to $S(Q, O) = p(O|Q, \Delta = 1) - p(O|Q, \Delta = 0)$.

- **Gaussian mixture model-based modeling**

  The pairwise view distance measures have a limitation that they neglect the structure information from multiple views for each object. Although the views are captured from different directions, they may possess similar structure information in feature space. To formulate the relationship among different views, we employ the Gaussian mixture model (GMM) to model the distribution of the views from one 3-D object [29]. We note that the number of views for each object is relatively small compared with the dimension of the feature. To address this problem, we first train a universal background model, which is a general GMM trained using all the views from the data set. Then, the views of one object are employed to adapt the universal background model to a specific GMM for the object. With the supervised information, such as relevance feedback from retrieval results, this GMM can be further adapted to be more discriminatory for the given object. With these generated GMMs, the distance between each pair of 3-D objects can be estimated using the Kullback-Leibler (KL) divergence between the two GMMs. Here, the upper bound of the KL divergence is employed as the approximation, since the KL divergence of GMMs is analytically intractable. This method benefits from general structure information, which can be represented from the GMMs, instead of using each single view.

1.4.5 Learning the Relevance Among 3-D Objects

As each 3-D object is represented by a group of views in V3DOR, it is difficult to estimate the relevance among 3-D objects by directly employing a pairwise distance measure. The pairwise distance measures, such as the Hausdorff distance [30, 31] and the earth mover's distance [32], are effective when two objects belonging to the same category share several close views. However, in V3DOR, it is not mandatory that objects belong to the same category. In addition, these methods may ignore the high-order relationship among objects with multiple views. For instance, it is difficult to determine which three objects share similar views when using the Hausdorff distance, which is based on the pairwise distance. The underlying relationship among all 3-D objects should be investigated to determine the overall similarity measure. We accordingly proposed learning-based 3DOR methods, which are briefly introduced below.

- **Hausdorff distance learning**

  Directly employing the Hausdorff distance for V3DOR does not produce a satisfactory result. This fact is due to the inaccurate distance measure between two views. For instance, some features may not be important and they should be downweighted to reduce their influence. It can be regarded as a way of distance metric learning, which is a general problem in many classification tasks. We note that it is difficult to optimize the Hausdorff distance metric for V3DOR because the relevance relationship is on the object level, while the distance metric is based on view pairs. To address this problem, we proposed a Hausdorff distance learning scheme for interactive V3DOR [33]. A set of labeled samples is collected with user relevance feedback from previous retrieval results. In the learning process, training view pairs from the labeled objects are probabilistically selected, including positive and negative view pair samples. A Mahalanobis distance metric for the view distance measure is learned with the training samples, which can be further employed in the object-level Hausdorff distance measure. We repeat the process and the matched view pairs from each pair of objects can be updated to learn an optimal distance metric. In this way, the optimal Hausdorff distance can be more effective on 3DOR.

- **Learning bipartite graph optimal matching**
  In our bipartite graph matching framework, one key issue is measuring the pairwise distance between two views, which is used to calculate the edges. With this goal in mind, we proposed a bipartite graph-matching, metric-learning algorithm in [34]. In this method, all objects are formulated in one (object) graph and each vertex denotes one object in the data set. For the edge between each pair of vertices, the bipartite graph matching-based similarity is calculated and the distance between each of the two views is measured according to the Mahalanobis distance. Given the query object, semi-supervised learning is conducted in the object graph, which jointly optimizes the relevance among all objects and the Mahalanobis distance for bipartite graph matching. This method benefits from the joint learning process, which incorporates the relationship among objects and the distance measure for bipartite graph construction, and these factors are important for constructing the graph.

- **Hypergraph learning**
  To model the high-order information of multiple views for 3-D objects, we formulated the relevance among 3-D objects using the hypergraph structure [35], which is not based on the pairwise distance measure. In this method, a hypergraph is constructed using the K-means view clustering results, in which each vertex denotes one object and each view cluster generates one hyperedge to connect the objects that have views in the cluster. The weight of each edge is defined using the visual similarities between any two views in the cluster. Because it is difficult to achieve

optimal view clustering, we conduct view clustering several times by varying the number of clusters in the K-means method used to generate multiple hypergraphs, which are able to actually encode the relationships among objects with different granularities. All these hypergraphs are combined to illustrate the object relevance structure in the data set. Semi-supervised learning is conducted on this fused hypergraph to estimate the relevance among 3-D objects. The multiple hypergraphs can be further optimally combined using learned coefficients with the user relevance feedback.

1.5 STRUCTURE OF THIS BOOK

The structure of this book is shown in Figure 1.2 and the remainder of this work is briefly introduced here.

- **Chapter 2. The benchmark**
  Given the rapid development of the 3DOR field, there are many public benchmarks available. In this chapter, we introduce several widely employed benchmarks, including the Princeton Shape Benchmark (PSB) [36], the Engineering Shape Benchmark (ESB) [37], the ITI database [38], the Amsterdam Library of Object Images (ALOI) [39], the Eidgenössische Technische Hochschule Zürich (ETH) data set [40], and the National Taiwan University (NTU) 3-D model data set [41]. We also introduce the recent 3DOR contest, the Shape Retrieval Contest (SHREC) [42].

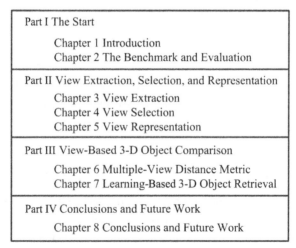

Part I The Start

    Chapter 1 Introduction
    Chapter 2 The Benchmark and Evaluation

Part II View Extraction, Selection, and Representation

    Chapter 3 View Extraction
    Chapter 4 View Selection
    Chapter 5 View Representation

Part III View-Based 3-D Object Comparison

    Chapter 6 Multiple-View Distance Metric
    Chapter 7 Learning-Based 3-D Object Retrieval

Part IV Conclusions and Future Work

    Chapter 8 Conclusions and Future Work

Figure 1.2 The structure of this book.

- **Chapter 3. View extraction**

  In this chapter, we introduce existing view extraction methods, which are based on different camera array settings. In this chapter, we also introduce our view generation method, that is, SSCD [24], which can preserve the global information of 3-D objects in 2-D images.

- **Chapter 4. View selection**

  Given the multiple views, view selection is an important procedure to select representative views and reduce redundancy. View selection methods can be generally divided into two categories, that is, a predefined camera array and view selection from the pool of views. In this chapter, we briefly review these two types of methods. We also introduce our proposed interactive QVS method [25], which employs user relevance feedback to incrementally select discriminatory views and determine the optimal distance metric.

- **Chapter 5. View representation**

  This chapter introduces the feature extraction methods in V3DOR. Many existing features have been employed in state-of-the-art methods and have been shown to be effective for view representation. In this chapter, we briefly review these widely employed features, such as Zernike moments [43], Krawtchouk moments [44], and the Fourier descriptor. Recently, the bag-of-visual-features descriptor [45–47] has been employed in V3DOR. Another important task in view representation relates to the weights of multiple views. We introduce our work on determining the weights by the graph propagation method in the last part of this chapter.

- **Chapter 6. Multiple-view distance metric**

  Matching two 3-D objects with multiple views is a key task of V3DOR. In this chapter, we first briefly introduce existing fundamental distance measures. Then, we introduce our bipartite graph matching-based method, which formulates two objects in a bipartite graph structure. The statistical matching methods in V3DOR are also introduced, including probabilistic matching using adaptive-view clustering and our probabilistic matching method using both positive and negative matching models. In the last part of this chapter, we introduce our GMM formulation for V3DOR, in which multiple GMMs are trained for 3-D object modeling.

- **Chapter 7. Learning-based 3-D object retrieval**

  To jointly explore the underlying structure from both the labeled and unlabeled 3-D objects and overcome the limitation of pairwise distance measures, we proposed several learning-based V3DOR methods. In this chapter, we introduce three methods, including Hausdorff distance

learning, learning for bipartite graph matching, and hypergraph learning methods in V3DOR.
- **Chapter 8. Conclusions and future work**
  We present our conclusions in this chapter. We summarize the themes of recent V3DOR research and examine the limitations of these studies. We also discuss how to further improve V3DOR performance and use V3DOR in real-world applications.

1.6 SUMMARY

In this chapter, we introduce the basic ideas and background of 3DOR, particularly V3DOR. We also compare the two categories of existing 3DOR methods, i.e., M3DOR and V3DOR. The challenges in V3DOR are also discussed. We summarize our studies and contributions in V3DOR and present the organization of this book.

REFERENCES

[1] Rui Y, Huang TS, Chang SF. Image retrieval: current techniques, promising directions, and open issues. J Vis Commun Image Represent 1999;10(1):39-62.

[2] Smeulders AW, Worring M, Santini S, Gupta A, Jain R. Content-based image retrieval at the end of the early years. IEEE Trans Pattern Anal Mach Intell 2000;22(12):1349-80.

[3] Datta R, Joshi D, Li J, Wang JZ. Image retrieval: ideas, influences, and trends of the new age. ACM Comput Surv 2008;40(2):5.

[4] Gunn TG. The mechanization of design and manufacturing. Sci Am 1982;247:114-30.

[5] Bustos B, Keim D, Saupe D, Schreck T. Content-based 3D object retrieval. IEEE Comput Graph Appl 2007;27(4):22-7.

[6] Bimbo AD, Pala PS. Content-based retrieval of 3D models. ACM Trans Multimed Comput Commun Appl 2007;2(1):20-43.

[7] Tangelder JWH, Veltkamp RC. A survey of content based 3D shape retrieval methods. Multimed Tools Appl 2008;39:441-71.

[8] Yang Y, Lin H, Zhang Y. Content-based 3-D model retrieval: a survey. IEEE Trans Syst Man Cybern Part C Appl Rev 2007;37:1081-35.

[9] Osada R, Funkhouser T, Chazelle B, Dobkin D. Shape distributions. ACM Trans Graph 2002;21(4):807-32.

[10] Paquet E, Murching A, Naveen T, Tabatabai A, Rioux M. Description of shape information for 2-D and 3-D objects. Signal Process Image Commun 2000;16: 103-22.

[11] Ip C, Lapadat D, Soeger L, Regli WC. Using shape distributions to compare solid models. In: Proc. ACM Symposium on Solid Modeling and Applications; 2002. p. 273-80.

[12] Johnson AE, Hebert M. Using spin images for efficient object recognition in cluttered 3D scenes. IEEE Trans Pattern Anal Mach Intell 1999;21(5):433-49.

[13] Makadia A, Daniilidis K. Spherical correlation of visual representations for 3D model retrieval. Int J Comput Vis 2010;89(2):193-210.

[14] Pajarola R, Sainz M, Guidotti P. Confetti: object-space point blending and splatting. IEEE Trans Vis Comput Graph 2004;10(5):598-608.

[15] Paquet E, Rioux M. Nefertiti: a tool for 3-D shape databases management. Image Vis Comput 2000;108:387-93.

[16] Tangelder J, Veltkamp R. Polyhedral model retrieval using weighted point sets. Int J Image Graph 2003;3(1):209-29.

[17] Funkhouser T, Min P, Kazhdan M, Chen J, Halderman A, Dobkin D, et al. A search engine for 3D models. ACM Trans Graph 2003;22(1):83-105.

[18] Sundar H, Silver D, Gagvani N, Dickinson SJ. Skeleton based shape matching and retrieval. In: Proceedings of the Shape Modeling International; 2003. p. 130-42.

[19] Zhang S, Yang M, Cour T, Yu K, Metaxas DN. Query specific fusion for image retrieval. Eur Conf Comput Vis 2012;2:660-73.

[20] Zhang S, Huang J, Li H, Metaxas DN. Automatic image annotation and retrieval using group sparsity. IEEE Trans Syst Man Cybern Part B 2012;42(3):838-49.

[21] Daras P, Axenopoulos A. A 3D shape retrieval framework supporting multimodal queries. Int J Comput Vis 2010;89(2):229-47.

[22] Bustos B, Keim D, Saupe D, Schreck T, Vranic D. Feature-based similarity search in 3D object databases. ACM Comput Surv 2005;37(4):345-87.

[23] Shilane P, Min P, Kazhdan M, Funkhouser T. The Princeton shape benchmark. In: Proceedings of Shape Modeling International; 2004. p. 167-78.

[24] Gao Y, Dai QH, Zhang NY. 3D model comparison using spatial structure circular descriptor. Pattern Recogn 2010;43(3):1142-51.

[25] Gao Y, Wang M, Zha Z, Tian Q, Dai Q, Zhang N. Less is more efficient 3D object retrieval with query view selection. IEEE Trans Multimed 2011;11(5):1007-18.

[26] Gao Y, Wang M, Ji R, Zha Z, Shen J. K-partite graph reinforcement and its application in multimedia information retrieval. Inf Sci 2012;194:224-39.

[27] Gao Y, Dai Q, Wang M, Zhang N. 3D model retrieval using weighted bipartite graph matching. Signal Process Image Commun 2011;26(1):39-47.

[28] Gao Y, Tang J, Hong R, Yan S, Dai Q, Zhang N, et al. Camera constraint-free view-based 3D object retrieval. IEEE Trans Image Process 2012;21(4):2269-81.

[29] Wang M, Gao Y, Lu K, Rui Y. View-based discriminative probabilistic modeling for 3D object retrieval and recognition. IEEE Trans Image Process 2013;22(4):1395-407.

[30] Atallah MJ. A linear time algorithm for the Hausdorff distance between convex polygons. Inf Process Lett 1983;17:207-9.

[31] Dubuisson MP, Jain AK. Modified Hausdorff distance for object matching. In: Proceedings of the IAPR International Conference on Pattern Recognition; 1994. p. 566-8.

[32] Rubner Y, Tomasi C, Guibas LJ. The earth mover's distance as a metric for image retrieval. Int J Comput Vis 2000;40(2):99-121.

[33] Gao Y, Wang M, Ji R, Wu X, Dai Q. 3D object retrieval with Hausdorff distance learning. IEEE Trans Ind Electron 2014;61(4):2088-98.

[34] Lu K, Ji R, Tang J, Gao Y. Learning-based bipartite graph matching for view-based 3D model retrieval. IEEE Trans Image Process 2014;23(10):4553-63.

[35] Gao Y, Wang M, Tao D, Ji R, Dai Q. 3D object retrieval and recognition with hypergraph analysis. IEEE Trans Image Process 2012;21(9):4290-303.

[36] Shilane P, Min P, Kazhdan M, Funkhouser T. The Princeton shape benchmark. In: Proceedings of Shape Modeling International; 2004. p. 167-78.

[37] Jayanti S, Kalyanaraman K, Iyer N, Ramani K. Developing an engineering shape benchmark for CAD models. Comput Aided Des 2004;38(9):939-53.

[38] Daras P, Tzovaras D, Dobravec S, Trnkoczy J, Sanna A, Paravati G, et al. Victory: a 3D search engine over P2P and wireless P2P networks. In: Proceedings of the 4th Annual International Conference on Wireless Internet; 2008. p. 49.

[39] Geusebroek J, Burghouts GJ, Smeulders AWM. The Amsterdam Library of Object Images. Int J Comput Vis 2005;61(1):103-12.

[40] Leibe B, Schiele B. Analyzing appearance and contour based methods for object categorization. In: Proceedings of IEEE International Conference on Computer Vision and Pattern Recognition; 2003. p. 409-15.

[41] Chen DY, Tian XP, Shen YT, Ouhyoung M. On visual similarity based 3D model retrieval. Comput Graph Forum 2003;22(3):223-32.

[42] http://www.aimatshape.net/event/SHREC/.

[43] Khotanzad A, Hong YH. Invariant image recognition by Zernike moments. IEEE Trans Pattern Anal Mach Intell 1990;12(5):489-97.

[44] Yap PT, Paramesran R, Ong SH. Image analysis by Krawtchouk moments. IEEE Trans Image Process 2003;12(11):1367-77.

[45] Ohbuchi R, Furuya T. Accelerating bag-of-features sift algorithm for 3D model retrieval. In: Proceedings of SAMT Workshop on Semantic 3D Media; 2008.

[46] Furuya T, Ohbuchi R. Dense sampling and fast encoding for 3D model retrieval using bag-of-visual features. In: Proceedings of the ACM International Conference on Image and Video Retrieval; 2009.

[47] Ohbuchi R, Osada K, Furuya T, Banno T. Salient local visual features for shape based 3D model retrieval. In: Proceedings of IEEE Conference on Shape Modeling and Applications; 2008. p. 93-102.

CHAPTER 2

The Benchmark and Evaluation

2.1 INTRODUCTION

Given the array of available applications, 3-D shape representation and matching and retrieval algorithms have been extensively investigated. These methods require standard benchmarks to evaluate their performance. Standard benchmarks are important for justifying the effectiveness of different method, and many 3-D object benchmarks have been released in recent years.

In this chapter, we review several popular 3-D benchmarks, including the Princeton Shape Benchmark (PSB) [1], the Engineering Shape Benchmark (ESB) [2], the ITI database [3], the Amsterdam Library of Object Images (ALOI) [4], the Eidgenössische Technische Hochschule (ETH) [5], and the National Taiwan University (NTU) [6] 3-D data sets. We also introduce the recent 3DOR contest, SHREC, on each year, respectively.

Evaluation methods are important to judge the performance of 3DOR. In the last part of this chapter, we introduce several widely used 3DOR retrieval performance evaluation criteria.

2.2 THE STANDARD BENCHMARKS

In this section, we introduce six standard benchmarks.

- **Princeton shape benchmark**
  PSB was collected by Princeton University. PSB contains 1814 polygonal 3-D models, which are collected from the World Wide Web from 293 different Web domains. All these models are manually classified based on functions and forms and multiple semantic labels are annotated for each 3-D model. These labels belong to a hierarchical structure, which can reflect the semantic in different levels. For example, a 3-D model with an annotation of "aircraft" can be further divided into subclasses, such as "winged_vehicle aircraft," "balloon_vehicle aircraft," and "helicopter aircraft." PSB has been split into a training set and a testing set. The training set contains 907 models, and the testing set contains the other

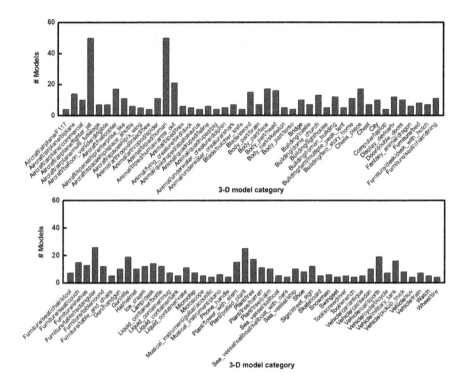

Figure 2.1 The distribution of different model categories in the PSB training set.

907 models. The distribution of all the models in PSB is shown in Figures 2.1 and 2.2. Example 3-D models from PSB are shown in Figure 2.3.

- **Engineering shape benchmark**

  ESB focuses on engineering shape representation. Computer-aided design product design is an iterative process, which is highly dependent on previous model designs. ESB aims to evaluate the shape representation to discriminate different shape forms for product design. ESB is composed of 867 3-D CAD models. For each 3-D model, there are CAD files, including two neutral formats: ".stl" and ".obj", and one thumbnail image. These models have been classified into three higher-level categories: *Flat-thin wall components*, *Rectangular-cubic prism*, and *Solids of revolution*. As introduced in [2], these three higher-level categories are defined as follows:

  - *Flat-thin wall components* are the parts with thin-walled sections and shell-like components.
  - *Rectangular-cubic prism* are the parts whose envelopes are largely rectangular or cubic prism.

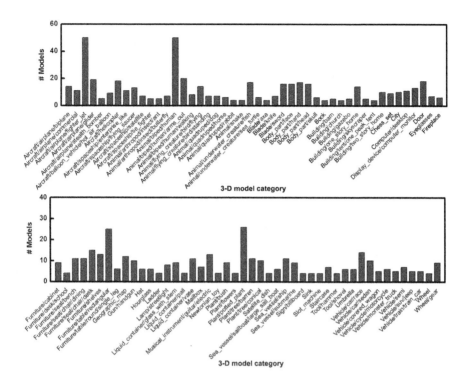

Figure 2.2 The distribution of different model categories in the PSB testing set.

Figure 2.3 Example 3-D models in PSB.

- *Solids of revolution* are the parts whose envelopes are largely solids of revolution.

These higher-level classes are further divided into 45 shape categories. The distribution of all the models in ESB is shown in Figure 2.4. Example 3-D models from ESB are shown in Figure 2.5.

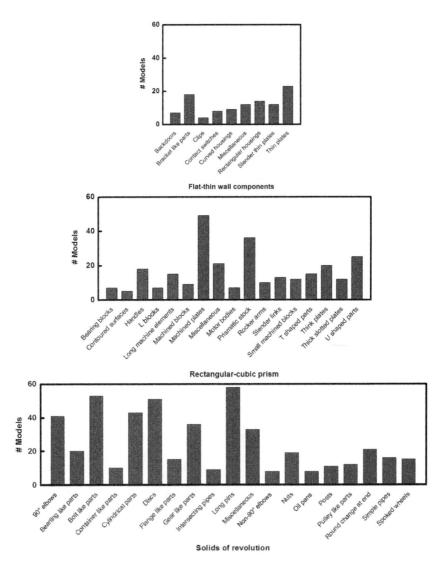

Figure 2.4 The distribution of different model categories in the ESB.

- **The ITI benchmark**
  The ITI data set is from the VICTORY 3-D search engineer [7]. The ITI data set contains 544 3-D models from 13 categories, including animals, spheroid objects, conventional airplanes, delta airplanes, helicopters, cars, motorcycles, tubes, couches, chairs, fish, humans, and some other models. Each 3-D model contains 5,080 vertices and 7,061 triangles on average. The distribution of all the models in the ITI data set is shown in Figure 2.6.

- **Amsterdam Library of Object Images**
  ALOI is a color image collection containing 1,000 small objects. We note that this data set does not provide the virtual 3-D model data, but only a set of images for each object. To obtain these images, the camera view angle, the illumination angle, and the illumination color for each object are systematically varied. For the camera view angle, the frontal camera is rotated in the plane at 5° to record 72 views of each object. For the illumination angle, there are eight different light conditions employed in the image data collection procedure, and five lights are employed. Each object is recorded with only one light turned on (five kinds in total), with only the left or right lights turned on (two kinds), and with all the lights turned on (one kind). Three cameras are employed to capture the views, which leads to a total of 24 different illumination conditions for recording views. The voltage of the lamps is varied 12 times for the illumination color, which yields 12 different illumination colors. Wide-baseline stereo images for 750 different scenarios are also recorded. In total, there are 110,250 images in the ALOI data set. Example objects from the ALOI benchmark are shown in Figure 2.7.

- **The Eidgenössische Technische Hochschule Zürich data set**
  The ETII benchmark contains 80 objects from eight categories and each category consists of 10 objects. These categories cover the following areas: fruits and vegetables, animals, small human-made objects, and large human-made objects. These eight categories include *apple, pear, tomato, cow, dog, horse, cup*, and *car*. In the ETH data set, a group of 41 views are recorded for each object. To capture these views, the object is placed on a table with blue chroma keying background and the views are obtained from directions spaced equally over the upper viewing hemisphere, subdividing an octahedron to the third recursion level. These views are recorded using a Sony DFW-X700 progressive scan digital camera at a resolution of 1024 × 768. For each view, the original color

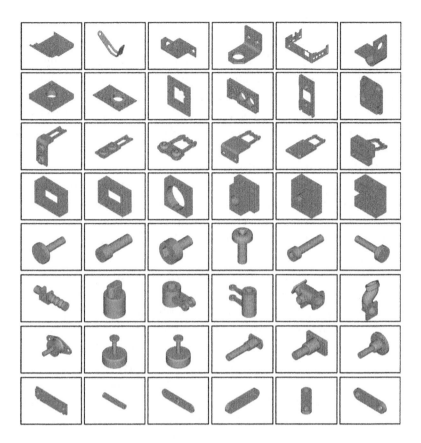

Figure 2.5 Example 3-D models in ESB.

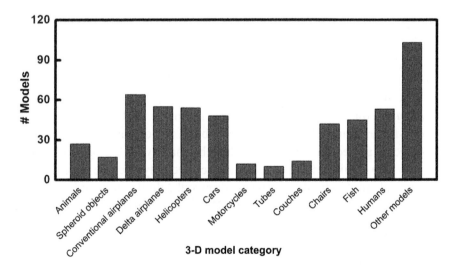

Figure 2.6 The distribution of different model categories in the ITI data set.

Figure 2.7 Example objects in the ALOI benchmark.

image and an associated high-quality segmentation mask are provided. Example objects from the ETH benchmark are shown in Figure 2.8.

- **The National Taiwan University data set**

  NTU contains two parts, the NTU 3-D model benchmark and the NTU 3-D model database. The NTU 3-D model benchmark consists of 1833 3-D models and the NTU 3-D model database consists of 10,911 3-D models. All these 3-D models are downloaded from the Internet in July 2002. These models are in Wavefront file format. For each model, a thumbnail image is provided in the data set. The NTU 3-D model bench-

Figure 2.8 Example objects in the ETH benchmark.

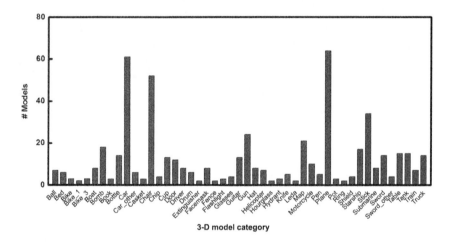

Figure 2.9 The distribution of different model categories in the NTU benchmark.

mark contains 47 categories with 549 3-D models, while another 1284 models are regarded as miscellaneous. The distribution of all models in the NTU 3-D model benchmark is shown in Figure 2.9, and example objects from the NTU 3-D model benchmark are shown in Figure 2.10.

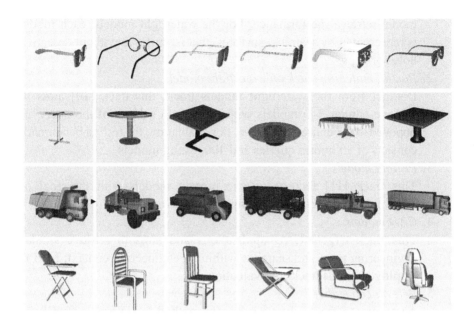

Figure 2.10 Example objects in the NTU benchmark.

2.3 THE SHAPE RETRIEVAL CONTEST

SHREC [8] is an annual contest that started from 2006. SHREC aims to evaluate the effectiveness of 3-D shape retrieval algorithms. Each year, different tracks are organized with various objectives and different testing benchmarks are employed or released. In this section, we briefly review the existing SHREC events, the employed benchmarks, and the challenging tasks.

• **SHREC2006**
  SHREC2006 is the first SHREC and there is only one task: retrieving a ranking list of similar 3-D objects given one query. In this contest, PSB is selected for performance evaluation.
• **SHREC2007**
  In SHREC2007, the tasks are classified into seven tracks, including the watertight models track, partial matching track on watertight models, protein models, CAD models, relevance feedback, similarity measures, and a shape retrieval contest of 3-D face models.
  1. *Watertight models track*
     The task in this track [9] is to retrieve watertight 3-D models. A testing benchmark with 500 watertight models is provided to evaluate 3-D

model retrieval performance. For the watertight models, each model is represented by seamless surfaces, that is, surfaces without defective holes or gaps.

2. *Partial matching track on watertight models*

Distinct from the watertight models track, this track [10] aims to retrieve similar 3-D models with a common subpart of the query, as opposed to the entire 3-D model. For evaluation, the testing benchmark consists of 30 hybrid queries and 400 testing models.

3. *Protein models*

This track [11] focuses on the protein models with the goal of searching for protein models similar to a given query.

4. *CAD models*

This track targets CAD applications and aims to retrieve similar engineering parts and searches within an engineering context. ESB is employed in this track for evaluation.

5. *Relevance feedback*

As relevance feedback is a powerful method for improving retrieval performance, the objective of this track is to evaluate the performance of different relevance feedback schemes in 3DOR. Two benchmarks—the ITI data set and PSB—are employed in this track.

6. *Similarity measures*

Similarity measures are important in 3DOR. This track focuses on new similarity measures for 3-D shape retrieval.

7. *Shape retrieval contest of 3-D face models*

3-D face models are targeted for this track. The goal is to retrieve a ranked list of 3-D face models given a query 3-D face. The testing benchmark consists of 1,000 morphable face models.

- **SHREC2008**

  SHREC2008 is composed of five tracks, including stability on watertight models, classification of watertight models, CAD models, generic 3-D models, and shape retrieval contest of 3-D face scans.

  1. *Stability on watertight models*

  The objective of this track [12] is to evaluate the stability of 3-D shape retrieval algorithms with different perturbations, such as geometric noise, small shape deformations, and varied sampling patterns.

  2. *Classification of watertight models*

  The main task in this track is a classification problem. This track [13] aims to assign an unknown 3-D model to predefined classes, in which the data are watertight 3-D models.

3. *CAD models*

Similar to the CAD models task in SHREC2007, this track [14] also focuses on CAD model retrieval, following the contest from the previous year.

4. *Generic 3-D models*

Generic 3-D models are the target in this track [15], which aims to retrieve similar generic 3-D models given a query model. This track represents the first SHREC attempt at generic 3-D model retrieval, which will be further explored in the subsequent SHREC events.

5. *Shape retrieval contest of 3-D face scans*

The objective of this track [16] is to retrieve similar 3-D face scans given a query 3-D face. The evaluation benchmark is a subset of GavabDB [17], which consists of 61 subjects. Seven different scans for these 61 subjects are selected and all 437 of these scans can be employed as the query. This track marks the first attempt to evaluate 3DOR methods on scan data, which explicitly represents 3-D information with depth scans.

- **SHREC2009**

A new track, 3-D retrieval using machine learning, is originated from SHREC2009. SHREC2009 includes four tracks: generic retrieval from a new benchmark, partial shape retrieval, 3-D retrieval using machine learning, and structural shape retrieval.

1. *Generic retrieval on new benchmark*

This task [18] aims to evaluate 3-D shape retrieval performance from a new 3-D shape benchmark. This new generic benchmark consists of 800 3-D models, which have been split into a query set and a data set. The query set contains 80 models belonging to 40 classes, where each class has two query models. The data set contains 720 models belonging to 40 classes, where each class has 18 models. In the contest, the query set is employed as the input and the retrieval process is conducted in the data set.

2. *Partial shape retrieval*

Following the partial matching track in SHREC2007, this track [19] aims to evaluate the partial similarity between the query model and the target models, particularly when the query is a depth map. The evaluation benchmark consists of two query sets and one target set. The first query set contains 20 3-D partial models and the second query set contains 20 range images. The target set contains 720 3-D models belonging to 40 classes, where each class has 18 models. The contest is based on different query types for partial shape retrieval.

3. *3-D retrieval using machine learning*

Machine learning has been extensively explored in recent years and is still rapidly developing. Considering recent progress in machine learning technologies, the objective of this track is to investigate machine learning-based 3DOR methods and to evaluate the performance and influence of different machine learning methods on 3-D model retrieval, including unsupervised learning algorithms and offline supervised learning algorithms. PSB is employed for evaluation in this track.

4. *Structural shape retrieval*

The structure information of 3-D models is employed in this track [20] as criteria for 3-D model comparisons. This technique differs from traditional semantical similarity. The testing benchmark consists of 200 3-D models, which are categorized into 10 main classes. Each main class is composed of two subclasses, where each subclass contains 10 3-D models. The hierarchical structure is employed as the groundtruth and also as the criteria for 3-D model retrieval.

- **SHREC2010**

In SHREC2010, new challenges are added, such as robustness, large-scale issue, and architectural models. SHREC2010 consists of 10 tracks, including range scans, nonrigid shapes, generic 3-D warehouse, protein models, correspondences, feature detection and description, robustness, face scans, large-scale retrieval and architectural models.

1. *Range scans*

This task [21] aims to retrieve relevant 3-D models given a range scan as the query. The evaluation benchmark consists of a query set and a target set. The query set contains 120 range images, which are captured from 40 models with three different ranges. The target set is composed of 800 3-D models, which are categorized into 40 classes.

2. *Nonrigid shapes*

Nonrigid shapes are ubiquitous in everyday life, from the macro level to the nano level. The objective of this track [22] is to retrieve similar 3-D models from a nonrigid data set. The testing benchmark consists of 200 models from the McGill Articulated Shape Benchmark of nonrigid 3-D models.

3. *Generic 3-D warehouse*

The focus on generic 3-D model retrieval is continued in this track [23], which aims to evaluate the performance of 3-D shape retrieval methods on a generic 3-D shape benchmark based on the Google 3-D Warehouse.

4. *Protein models*

Similar to the Protein Retrieval Challenge in [11], this track [24] continues to focus on protein model retrieval.

5. *Correspondences*

Optimal correspondences with the structure preservation criterion can be regarded as a criterion for shape similarity. The correspondence between two shapes can be invariant to shape transformations, which can be robust to shape retrieval. This track [25] aims to evaluate the performance of algorithms related to establishing a correspondence between two shapes.

6. *Feature detection and description*

Feature extraction is important for 3-D shape retrieval. A variety of feature extraction methods exist and this track [26] aims to evaluate the performance of shape feature and descriptors with varied transformations.

7. *Robustness*

The robustness of 3-D shape retrieval confronts challenges of the rotation and translation of rigid shapes, deformations of nonrigid shapes, connectivity and topological changes, holes and noise of scanned shapes, and missing parts, different sampling, and triangulations of other data. The objective of this track is to evaluate the performance of shape retrieval methods under varied transformations.

8. *Face scans*

Similar to the shape retrieval contest of 3-D face scans in [16], this track continues to focus on 3-D face scan retrieval, in which the scanned data are employed for processing.

9. *Large-scale retrieval*

Large data sets are a common challenge in multimedia information retrieval. This track [27] aims to investigate effective and efficient methods for dealing with large amounts of 3-D model data. The generic benchmark released in this track is composed of 10,000 3-D models from different categories, among which about 40 models are employed as queries.

10. *Architectural models*

An architectural model is one important type of data for design. The objective of this track is to evaluate the performance of 3-D shape retrieval methods on architectural models. The benchmark consists of 2,000 models, including 50 queries. These models consist of objects located in or around the household, including lighting, furniture, and technical materials.

- **SHREC2011**

  SHREC2011 continues seven tasks from SHREC2010, including the shape retrieval contest of range scans, nonrigid shapes, the generic 3-D warehouse, correspondences, feature detection and description, robustness, and face scans.

  1. *Shape retrieval contest of range scans*

     The objective of this track follows SHREC2010, while the data set is updated. The benchmark is composed of a query set and a target set. The query set consists of 150 range images from 50 classes with three range scan data. The target set contains 1,000 3-D models from 50 classes.

  2. *Nonrigid shapes*

     The objective of this track [28] is similar to that in SHREC2010, while the benchmark is composed of 600 nonrigid 3-D models compared with 200 models in SHREC2010.

  3. *Generic 3-D warehouse*

     The objective of this track [29] is similar to that in SHREC2010, while the benchmark is composed of 1,000 3-D models from 50 classes.

  4. *Correspondences*

     The objective of this track is similar to that in SHREC2010 and targets the evaluation of the performance of algorithms based on the correspondence between two shapes.

  5. *Feature detection and description*

     The objective of this track [30] is similar to that in SHREC2010. This track evaluates the performance of shape feature and descriptors with varied transformations.

  6. *Robustness*

     The objective of this track is the same as the task in SHREC2010, that is, evaluating the performance of shape retrieval methods with varied transformations.

  7. *Face scans*

     Similar to the tasks in SHREC2008 and SHREC2010, the objective of this track [31] is to retrieve similar 3-D face scans given a specific query. The benchmark is composed of a training set and a testing set. The training set contains 60 models of Roland scans, and the testing set contains 580 Escans and 70 Roland scans.

- **SHREC2012**

  Three new contests are presented in SHREC2012. The contest is composed of four tracks: 3-D mesh segmentation, stability with respect to abstract shapes, sketch-based 3-D shape retrieval, and generic 3-D model retrieval.

1. *3-D mesh segmentation*

   Distinct from the previous retrieval-based task, the objective of this track [32] is to segment the 3-D models, that is, segment each model into meaningful components. The semantic components can be very helpful for other tasks, such as retrieval, recognition, and annotation. The evaluation benchmark consists of 28 watertight models from five classes, including animals, furniture, hands, humans, and busts.

2. *Stability on abstract shapes*

   This track focuses on abstract shapes. The objective of this track [33] is to evaluate the stability of different algorithms according to variations in abstract shapes.

3. *Sketch-based 3-D shape retrieval*

   Sketch-based research has attracted significant attention in recent years. This track [34] aims to evaluate the performance of sketch-based, 3-D model retrieval algorithms. In this task, both hand-drawn and standard line drawing sketch can be the queries for a watertight 3-D model benchmark.

4. *Generic 3-D model retrieval*

   Similar to the contests from previous years, this track [35] aims to evaluate the performance of generic 3-D model retrieval algorithms. The evaluation benchmark is composed of 1,200 3-D models from 60 categories.

- **SHREC2013**

  SHREC2013 is composed of four tracks, including large-scale partial shape retrieval using simulated range images, retrieval of objects captured with low-cost depth-sensing cameras, retrieval of textured 3-D models, and large-scale sketch-based 3-D shape retrieval.

  1. *Large-scale partial shape retrieval using simulated range images*

     The objective of this track is to evaluate the performance of 3-D model retrieval algorithms with range images. For each 3-D model, a partial scan is simulated by generating point clouds from multiple views of the model. The evaluation benchmark consists of a query set and a target set. The query set includes 360 models from 20 classes that are selected from the Generic Retrieval Benchmark in SHREC2009. Twenty partial views are obtained from each model. There are accordingly 7,200 queries in total. The target set contains the same 360 models.

2. *Retrieval of objects captured with low-cost depth-sensing cameras*
   The objective of this track is to evaluate the performance of 3-D model retrieval algorithms with a commodity low-cost depth scanner. The evaluation benchmark is composed of 192 models captured using a Microsoft® Kinect camera.
3. *Retrieval on textured 3-D models*
   The objective of this track is to evaluate the performance of 3-D model retrieval algorithms with varied geometric shapes and texture conditions. The evaluation benchmark is composed of 240 textured shapes from 10 classes.
4. *Large-scale sketch-based 3-D shape retrieval*
   This track [36] aims to evaluate the performance of 3-D model retrieval algorithms with large-scale hand-drawn sketch queries. The evaluation benchmark is generated from PSB, which is composed of 7,200 sketches and 1,258 3-D models from 90 classes.

2.4 EVALUATION CRITERIA IN 3DOR

For 3DOR, evaluation criteria are important to evaluate the performance of different methods. Generally, given a query image, a 3DOR method can calculate the distance or similarity with other objects in the testing data set. Given the final ranking list of retrieved 3-D objects, several widely used evaluation criteria have been introduced to justify the performance of 3DOR methods. In this section, we introduce these evaluation criteria, including precision, recall, precision-recall (PR) curve, F-measure [37], first tier (FT), second tier (ST), nearest-neighbor precision, discounted cumulative gain (DCG) [38, 39], and average normalized modified retrieval rank (ANMRR) [40].

- **Precision**. The precision criteria measure the precision of retrieved objects. The precision can be defined as follows:

$$\text{Precision} = \frac{\#\{(\text{relevant objects}) \cap (\text{retrieved objects})\}}{\#(\text{retrieved objects})}, \qquad (2.1)$$

where {(relevant objects)} are the relevant objects for the query (the groundtruth), {(retrieved objects)} are the retrieved objects given the query, and $\#(X)$ is the number of objects in X. The precision value ranges from 0 to 1. For a perfect retrieval result, the precision value is 1, which indicates that all the retrieved results are correct.

- **Recall**. The recall criteria measures the recall of retrieved objects compared with the groundtruth. The recall can be defined as follows:

$$\text{Recall} = \frac{\#\{(\text{relevant objects}) \cap (\text{retrieved objects})\}}{\#(\text{relevant objects})}. \qquad (2.2)$$

The recall value ranges from 0 to 1. For a perfect retrieval result, the recall value is 1, which indicates that all the relevant objects have been correctly retrieved.

- **Precision-recall curve**. The PR curve is a plot that describes the relationship between the precision and the recall according to a ranking list. For a good retrieval result, the PR curve should be as close to the upper-right corner of the plot as possible, which indicates high precision with high recall.

- **F-1 measure**. The F-1 measure [37] is a composite measure of both the precision and the recall for a fixed number of returned results. For example, the F-1 measure can be set to 32 because the returned results in the first page are more important than others. The F-1 measure is defined as

$$F1 = \frac{2 \times P_K \times R_K}{P_K \times R_K}, \qquad (2.3)$$

where K is the number of selected top returned results, P_K is the precision for the top K results, and R_K is the recall for the top K results. For perfect retrieval results, the F-1 measure is 1. A higher F-1 measure value indicates a better retrieval performance.

- **First tier**. FT is a measure of the recall of the top results, where the number of selected retrieved results is equal to the number of all relevant objects in the data set. FT is calculated according to

$$\text{FT} = \frac{\#(\text{relevant objects at top } \tau \text{ results})}{\#(\text{relevant objects})}, \qquad (2.4)$$

where τ is the number of relevant samples in the entire data set and $\#(X)$ is the number of objects in X.

- **Second tier**. ST also measures the recall in the top results and is defined by

$$\text{ST} = \frac{\#(\text{relevant objects at top } 2 \times \tau \text{ results})}{\#(\text{relevant objects})}, \qquad (2.5)$$

where $\#(\text{relevant objects at top } 2 \times \tau \text{ results})$ is the number of relevant objects in the top $2 \times \tau$ retrieved results.

- **Nearest-neighbor precision.** Nearest-neighbor precision (P1) measures the retrieval accuracy of the first returned result.
- **Discounted cumulative gain.** DCG [38, 39] is a statistical measure that assigns higher weights to relevant results occupying the top-ranking positions. DCG works under the assumption that a user is less like to consider lower results. The DCG value for the first returned result is calculated according to

$$DCG_1 = \delta(1), \tag{2.6}$$

and the DCG value for the ith returned result is calculated according to

$$DCG_i = DCG_{i-1} + \frac{\delta(1)}{\log_2(i)}, \tag{2.7}$$

where

$$\delta(i) = \begin{cases} 1 & \text{if the } i\text{th result is correct} \\ 0 & \text{otherwise} \end{cases}. \tag{2.8}$$

Assuming that the number of all relevant objects in a given query is τ and the number of all objects in the data set is n, the maximal DCG is calculated according to

$$DCG_{max} = \frac{DCG_n}{1 + \sum_{i=2}^{\tau} \frac{1}{\log_2(i)}}. \tag{2.9}$$

- **Average normalized modified retrieval rank.** ANMRR [40] measures the rank performance given a ranking list, which considers the ranking information of relevant objects among the top-retrieved objects. ANMRR ranges from 0 to 1 and a lower ANMRR value indicates a better retrieval performance.

  To calculate ANMRR, the average retrieval rank (ARR) is first introduced here. Given the kth query Q_k, the top $S_k = \min\{4 \times \tau_k, 2 \times \tau_{max}\}$ returned results are taken into consideration, where τ_k is the number of relevant objects for Q_k, and τ_{max} is the maximal number of relevant objects for all the queries. For these S_k objects, if the ith result is relevant to the query, the rank $r(i)$ is the ranking position; otherwise $r(i)=S+1$. The ARR is accordingly calculated as

$$ARR(Q_k) = \sum_{i=1}^{\tau_k} \frac{r(i)}{\tau_k}. \tag{2.10}$$

The modified retrieval rank (MRR) can be calculated according to

$$\text{MRR}(Q_k) = \text{ARR}(Q_k) - \frac{\tau_k}{2} - 0.5. \tag{2.11}$$

Then the MRR can be normalized to obtain the normalized MRR (NMRR) as

$$\text{NMRR}(Q_k) = \frac{\text{MRR}(Q_k)}{S_k - \frac{\tau_k}{2} + 0.5}. \tag{2.12}$$

The ANMRR can be obtained by averaging the NMRR values of all queries as

$$\text{ANMRR} = \frac{1}{n_q} \sum_{k=1}^{n_q} \text{NMRR}(Q_k), \tag{2.13}$$

where n_q is the number of queries.

2.5 SUMMARY

In this chapter, we have briefly reviewed existing 3-D model benchmarks for 3DOR. For some benchmarks, the 3-D model information is available and the depth data can be obtained. While for some benchmarks, only views are available, which means the depth data cannot be used. Given recent progress in depth image processing, 3DOR based on depth data is more powerful and has a wider range of applications. Therefore, large-scale 3-D object benchmarks with captured depth information, for example, by Microsoft® Kinect, are urgently needed. SHREC is introduced in this chapter, including the tasks and the benchmarks. Several evaluation criteria for 3DOR results have also been introduced in this chapter.

REFERENCES

[1] Shilane P, Min P, Kazhdan M, Funkhouser T. The Princeton shape benchmark. In: Proceedings of Shape Modeling International; 2004. p. 167-78.

[2] Jayanti S, Kalyanaraman K, Iyer N, Ramani K. Developing an engineering shape benchmark for CAD models. Comput Aided Des 2004;38(9):939-53.

[3] Daras P, Tzovaras D, Dobravec S, Trnkoczy J, Sanna A, Paravati G, et al. Victory: a 3D search engine over P2P and wireless P2P networks. In: Proceedings of the 4th Annual International Conference on Wireless Internet. No. 49; 2008.

[4] Geusebroek J, Burghouts GJ, Smeulders AWM. The Amsterdam Library of Object Images. Int J Comput Vis 2005;61(1):103-12.

[5] Leibe B, Schiele B. Analyzing appearance and contour based methods for object categorization. In: Proceedings of IEEE International Conference on Computer Vision and Pattern Recognition; 2003. p. 409-15.

[6] Chen DY, Tian XP, Shen YT, Ouhyoung M. On visual similarity based 3D model retrieval. Comput Graph Forum 2003;22(3):223-32.

[7] IST VICTORY project page. http://www.victory-eu.org.

[8] http://www.aimatshape.net/event/SHREC/.

[9] Giorgi D, Biasotti S, Paraboschi L. Shape retrieval contest 2007: watertight models track. In: Int. Conference on Shape Modeling and Applications; 2007.

[10] Marini S, Paraboschi L, Biasotti S. Shape retrieval contest 2007: partial matching track. In: Int. Conference on Shape Modeling and Applications; 2007.

[11] Temerinac M, Reisert M, Burkhardt H. SHREC07-protein retrieval challenge. In: Int. Conference on Shape Modeling and Applications; 2007.

[12] Biasotti S, Attene M. SHREC08 entry: report of the stability track on watertight models. In: Int. Conference on Shape Modeling and Applications; 2008.

[13] Giorgi D, Marini S. Shape retrieval contest 2008: classification of watertight models. In: Int. Conference on Shape Modeling and Applications; 2008.

[14] Muthuganapathy R, Ramani K. Shape retrieval contest 2008: CAD models. In: Int. Conference on Shape Modeling and Applications; 2008.

[15] Ohbuchi R. Shape retrieval contest 2008: generic models. In: Int. Conference on Shape Modeling and Applications; 2008.

[16] ter Haar FB, Veltkamp RC. SHREC08 entry: 3D face recognition using facial contour curves. In: Int. Conference on Shape Modeling and Applications; 2008.

[17] Moreno AB, Sánchez A. GavabDB: a 3D face database. In: Workshop on Biometrics on the Internet COST275, Vigo, March 25-26, 2004. p. 77-85.

[18] Godil A, Dutagaci H, Akgül C, Axenopoulos A, Bustos B, Chaouch M, et al. SHREC'09 track: generic shape retrieval. In: Proceedings of Eurographics Workshop on 3D Object Retrieval; 2009.

[19] Dutagaci H, Godil A, Axenopoulos A, Daras P, Furuya T, Ohbuchi R. SHREC'09 track: querying with partial models. In: Proceedings of Eurographics Workshop on 3D Object Retrieval; 2009.

[20] Hartveldt J, Spagnuolo M, Axenopoulos A, Biasotti S, Daras P, Dutagaci H, et al. SHREC'09 track: structural shape retrieval on watertight models. In: Proceedings of Eurographics Workshop on 3D Object Retrieval; 2009.

[21] Dutagaci H, Godil A, Cheung CP, Furuya T, Hillenbrand U, Ohbuchi R. SHREC'10 track: range scan retrieval. In: Proceedings of Eurographics Workshop on 3D Object Retrieval; 2010.

[22] Lian Z, Godil A, Furuya T, Hermans J, Ohbuchi R, Shu C, et al. SHREC10 track: non-rigid 3D shape retrieval. In: Proceedings of Eurographics Workshop on 3D Object Retrieval; 2010.

[23] Vanamali TP, Godil A, Dutagaci H, Furuya T, Lian Z, Ohbuchi R. SHREC'10 track: generic 3D warehouse. In: Proceedings of Eurographics Workshop on 3D Object Retrieval; 2010.

[24] Mavridis L, Venkatraman V, Ritchie DW, Morikawa N, Andonov R, Cornu A, et al. SHREC-10 track: protein models. In: Proceedings of Eurographics Workshop on 3D Object Retrieval; 2010.

[25] Bronstein A, Bronstein M, Castellani U, Dubrovina A, Guibas L, Horaud R, et al. SHREC 2010: robust correspondence benchmark. In: Proceedings of Eurographics Workshop on 3D Object Retrieval; 2010.

[26] Bronsteiny AM, Bronsteiny MM, Bustos B, Castellaniy U, Crisani M, Falcidieno B, et al. SHREC 2010: robust feature detection and description benchmark. In: Proceedings of Eurographics Workshop on 3D Object Retrieval; 2010.

[27] Bronstein AM, Bronstein MM, Castellani U, Falcidieno B, Fusiello A, Godil A, et al. SHREC 2010: robust large-scale shape retrieval benchmark. In: Proceedings of Eurographics Workshop on 3D Object Retrieval; 2010.

[28] Lian Z, Godil A, Bustos B, Daoudi M, Hermans J, Kawamura S, et al. SHREC'11 track: shape retrieval on non-rigid 3D watertight meshes. In: Proceedings of the 4th Eurographics Conference on 3D Object Retrieval; 2011. p. 79-88.

[29] Dutagaci H, Afzal G, Petros D, Apostolos A, Litos G, Manolopoulou S, et al. SHREC'11 track: Generic shape retrieval. In: Proceedings of the 4th Eurographics Conference on 3D Object Retrieval; 2011. p. 65-9.

[30] Boyer E, Bronstein AM, Bronstein MM, Bustos B, Darom T, Horaud R, et al. SHREC 2011: robust feature detection and description benchmark. In: Proceedings of the 4th Eurographics Conference on 3D Object Retrieval; 2011. p. 71-8.

[31] Veltkamp RC, Van Jole S, Drira H, Amor BB, Daoudi M, Li H, et al. SHREC'11 track: 3D face models retrieval. In: Proceedings of the 4th Eurographics Conference on 3D Object Retrieval; 2011. p. 89-95.

[32] Lavoué G, Vandeborre JP, Benhabiles H, Daoudi M, Huebner K, Mortara M, et al. SHREC'12 track: 3D mesh segmentation. In: Proceedings of the 5th Eurographics Conference on 3D Object Retrieval; 2012. p. 93-9.

[33] Biasotti S, Bai X, Bustos B, Cerri A, Giorgi D, Li L, et al. SHREC'12 track: stability on abstract shapes. In: Proceedings of the 5th Eurographics Conference on 3D Object Retrieval. Eurographics Association; 2012.

[34] Li B, Schreck T, Godil A, Alexa M, Boubekeur T, Bustos B, et al. SHREC'12 track: sketch-based 3D shape retrieval. In: Proceedings of the 5th Eurographics Workshop on 3D Object Retrieval; 2012.

[35] Li B, Godil A, Aono M, Bai X, Furuya T, Li L, et al. SHREC'12 track: generic 3D shape retrieval. In: Proceedings of the 5th Eurographics Workshop on 3D Object Retrieval; 2012.

[36] Li B, Lu Y, Godil A, Schreck T, Aono M, Johan H, et al. SHREC'13 track: large scale sketch-based 3D shape retrieval. In: Proceedings of the 5th Eurographics Workshop on 3D Object Retrieval; 2013. p. 89-96.

[37] van Rijsbergen CK. Information retrieval. London: Butterworths; 1975.

[38] Jarvelin K, Kekalainen J. Cumulated gain-based evaluation of IR techniques. ACM Trans Inf Syst 2002;20(4):422-66.

[39] Voorhees EM. Evaluation by highly relevant documents. In: Proceedings of the 24th ACM-SIGIR Conference on Research and Development in Information Retrieval; 2001. p. 74-82.

[40] Description of Core Experiments for MPEG-7 Color/Texture Descriptors, Standard ISO/MPEGJTC1/SC29/WG11 MPEG98/M2819; 1999.

PART II

View Extraction, Selection, and Representation

Data are the first challenge in all multimedia information retrieval tasks. The retrieval task can benefit from well-organized data and suffer from bad data, such as insufficient, redundant, and even incorrect information. In view-based 3-D object analysis, the data include the multiple views of each 3-D object. The challenges of data stem from three aspects: view extraction, view selection, and view representation. This part of the book focuses on the data and introduces recent works related to these three topics.

Chapter 3 introduces view extraction studies, including dense sampling viewpoint methods, predefined camera arrays, and generated views. Chapter 4 reviews the view selection methods from a pool of views. This Chapter is primarily composed of two types of methods: unsupervised view selection and interactive view selection. Chapter 5 discusses the view representation methods, including shape feature extraction, the bag-of-visual-features methods, and weight learning for multiple views.

CHAPTER *3*

View Extraction

3.1 INTRODUCTION

View extraction is the first step of V3DOR and is a required procedure. Each existing V3DOR method employs a commonly used or its self-designed view acquisition technique. A group of carefully obtained views forms a strong foundation for further V3DOR. As a result, effective view acquisition techniques are highly desired for 3-D applications.

Existing view extraction methods can be divided into three categories: dense sampling viewpoints, predefined camera arrays, and generated views. In dense view sampling methods, view acquisition is based on densely sampled view directions. The multiple views are densely collected from these directions. In predefined camera array methods, a camera array is first defined to obtain multiple view collection directions. For generated view methods, the views are generated from the 3-D object, as opposed to the direct images.

In this chapter, we briefly introduce the three types of existing view extraction methods, including the elevation descriptor (ED) [1], adaptive view clustering (AVC) [2], the compact multiple view descriptor (CMVD) [3], and panoramic views [4]. In the last part of this chapter, we introduce our spatial-structure circular descriptor (SSCD) [5] as a generated view method.

3.2 DENSE SAMPLING VIEWPOINTS

The dense sampling viewpoints method captures multiple views from the viewpoints, which are uniformly and regularly spread over the view sphere surrounding the 3-D object. The main advantage of this type of methods lies in its capability to gather complete data from all directions with no prior information. Typical dense sampling viewpoints methods include AVC [2] and the technique discussed in a study by Ohbuchi et al. [10].

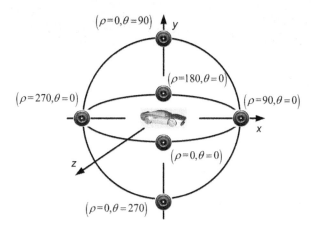

Figure 3.1 Illustration of dense sampling viewpoints in AVC.

In AVC [2], 320 views are gathered from the original 3-D model. A two-unit icosahedron is employed to capture these views. The icosahedron is further divided twice using the Loop subdivision scheme to produce a polyhedron with 320 facets. The viewpoints are located at the face centers of this polyhedron, which are densely sampled in the sphere pointing toward the 3-D object. Figure 3.1 illustrates the dense viewpoint directions in AVC.

Similar to AVC, 80 views are densely generated in [6, 7] by subdividing the icosahedron once using the Loop subdivision scheme.

Furuya and Ohbuchi [8–11] propose employing dense sampling viewpoints uniformly located on a view sphere that surrounds the 3-D model with 42 cameras. In this arrangement, all viewpoints are located at 80-face semiregular polyhedron generated from the icosahedron using butterfly subdivision with 42 vertices. The viewpoint directions are shown in Figure 3.2.

For the dense sampling viewpoints methods, the multiple obtained views can preserve a significant amount of information from intensive directions. The data are rich, but not compact, which means that an additional view selection process is required to reduce their redundancy.

3.3 PREDEFINED CAMERA ARRAY

In this type of methods predefined camera arrays are employed for view acquisition. In these methods, the views are not densely captured, which

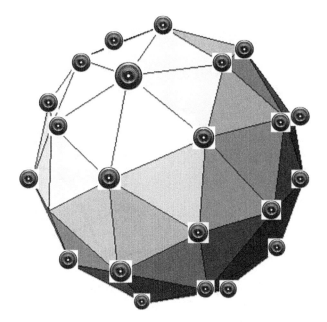

Figure 3.2 Illustration of the dense sampling viewpoints in studies by Ohbuchi and collaborators [8–11].

indicates that the view selection procedure has been involved in the camera array setting part and that no further view selection process is required.

A typical method using a camera array setting is the lighting field descriptor (LFD) [12]. In LFD, the cameras are located at the 20 vertices of a regular dodecahedron, that is, the 12-hedron. These cameras can gather 20 silhouettes. Because the two corresponding silhouettes that are projected from 2 opposite vertices on the dodecahedron are identical, 10 silhouettes are selected from this camera array. To reduce the influence of 3-D model rotation, the camera array has 20 × 3 different settings (20 vertices, each of which is connected by three edges). The 3-D model can also rotate a little. Ten positions of each 3-D model are employed to generate the LFDs and thus there are 10 groups of LFDs for each 3-D model. Figure 3.3 illustrates the camera array locations located on the vertices on a regular dodecahedron in a study by Chen et al. [12].

ED [1] employs a tight bounding box circumscribing the 3-D model to set the virtual cameras. The 3-D model is projected onto the six facets of the bounding box, that is, the front, rear, top, bottom, left, and right. Then, each 3-D model is described by six EDs, which are six gray images indicating altitude information. Figure 3.4 illustrates the viewpoint directions in [1].

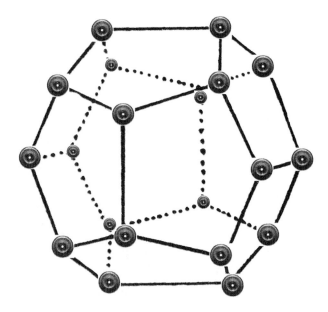

Figure 3.3 Illustration of the camera arrays located on the vertices of a regular dodecahedron in a study by Chen et al. [12].

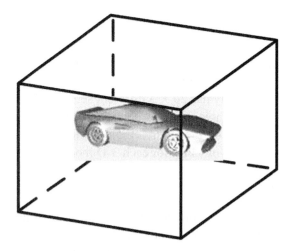

Figure 3.4 Illustration of the viewpoint directions in a study by Shih et al. [1].

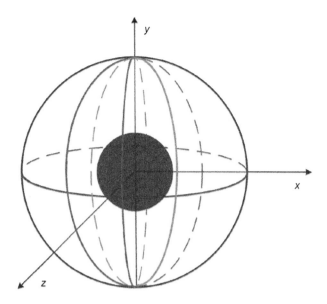

Figure 3.5 Illustration of the viewpoint directions in a study by Gao et al. [13].

CMVD [3] employs the 18 vertices of a 32-hedron to extract multiple views for 3-D model description. The orthographic projection is employed, in which two images are generated from each camera direction: the binary image and the depth image. The binary image records the locations of the 3-D object, and the depth image records the distance of the 3-D object to the projection plane.

Five circle camera arrays are employed in a study by Gao et al. [13]. One horizontal circle and four vertical circles in the sphere are employed to set the cameras, as shown in Figure 3.5. In each circle, two adjacent cameras have the same interval (18°). The 3-D model is located in the center of the sphere and the five groups of 2-D views are obtained by the camera arrays.

3.4 GENERATED VIEW

The third category of view acquisition methods generates one or more views from the initial 3-D model. As opposed to the previous two types of methods, which directly capture views using (virtual) cameras, this type of methods employ a photographic approach to generate views. The required 3-D descriptive view should preserve the spatial structure information.

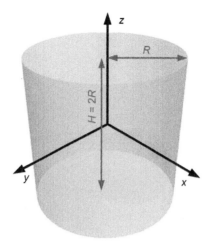

Figure 3.6 Illustration of the cylinder for the 3-D model projection acquisition in a study by Papadakis et al. [4].

A typical view generation method is the PANoramic Object Representation for Accurate Model Attributing (PANORAMA) [4]. In PANORAMA, the 3-D model position is first normalized. The model is projected onto the lateral surface of a cylinder. The cylinder is centered at the origin with a radius R and height $H = 2R$, where $R = 3d_{\mathrm{mean}}$, and d_{mean} is the average distance from each point in the 3-D model surface to the centroid. Figure 3.6 illustrates the cylinder for a 3-D model.

The cylindrical projection next obtains the position of the surface in 3-D space and the orientation of the surface. The distance from each surface point to the center at the same height is calculated as the projection for the position of surface points. The angle between a ray from the surface point and the normal vector is measured to capture the surface orientation. To capture the 3-D model information from different directions, three cylinders following the x-, y-, and z-axes in the pose normalization step, respectively, are used to generate the three projections.

We propose an SSCD in [5] for view generation. In SSCD, the spherical grade projection is employed to capture the surface information of one sphere. The spherical grade projection aims to project a sphere surface onto a plane. Given a point X in a sphere, the ray is oriented from the north polar and passes X with an intersection point Y on the project plane of the south polar. In this way, the spherical grade projection can project all the points in the sphere onto the projection plane. One point close to the north polar is associated with a corresponding intersection point that is far from the center. The spherical graph projection method has been used in the SSCD method. In the SSCD framework, a minimal bounding sphere is generated and all the points on the surface of the 3-D model are projected onto the bounding sphere, which generates a depth bounding sphere. In this depth bounding sphere, each point in the surface is associated with one or more corresponding attribute values that represent the spatial information of the model surface point from different layers. Next, the depth bounding sphere is further projected onto a circular region to represent the 3-D model information. The details are given as follows.

To generate the SSCD of a given 3-D model, a minimal bounding sphere is generated for the model. The origin is set as the centroid of the bounding sphere and r denotes the radius of the bounding sphere, as shown in Figure 3.7. The surface point in the 3-D model is projected onto the bounding sphere. Given a surface point $M(x_m, y_m, z_m)$, a ray oriented from the origin passes M and has an intersection point $S(x_s, y_s, z_s)$ with the bounding sphere. $S(x_s, y_s, z_s)$ can be generated as

$$\begin{cases} x_s^2 + y_s^2 + z_s^2 = r^2 \\ \dfrac{x_s}{x_m} = \dfrac{y_s}{y_m} = \dfrac{z_s}{z_m} \end{cases} \tag{3.1}$$

The depth information a_s of the bounding sphere point S for M is calculated according to

$$a_s = \theta_m \times d_m / r, \tag{3.2}$$

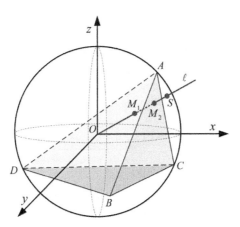

Figure 3.7 The illustration of depth bounding sphere projection in SSCD [5].

$$d_{\mathrm{m}} = \sqrt{x_{\mathrm{m}}^2 + y_{\mathrm{m}}^2 + z_{\mathrm{m}}^2}, \tag{3.3}$$

where d_{m} is the Euclidian distance between M and the centroid of the 3-D model, and θ_{m} is a parameter of the surface type of M. As shown in   Figure 3.7, there are two types of surface points: M_1 and M_2. For M_1, the surface point faces toward the origin. For M_2, the surface point faces toward the bounding sphere. To note this difference, we employ the parameter θ_{m}, where $\theta_{\mathrm{m}} = 1$ for M_1 and $\theta_{\mathrm{m}} = -1$ for M_2. We find that if the ray makes multiple intersections with the model surface, that is, η, the corresponding depth sphere point will have more than one attribute value $a_{\mathrm{m}}(1), a_{\mathrm{m}}(2), \ldots, a_{\mathrm{m}}(\eta)$.

In the next step, the depth bounding sphere is projected onto a plane to generate the SSCD images, preserving the global spatial structure information of the 3-D model. We move the origin to the north polar of the depth bounding sphere. Figure 3.8 shows the projection procedure, in which C is the spherical center, the plane of OPS is orthogonal to the plane of XOY, and ϑ is the angle between CS and the Z-axis.

Given a surface point $S(x_{\mathrm{s}}, y_{\mathrm{s}}, z_{\mathrm{s}})$ on the depth bounding sphere, the projection should preserve the spatial structure of the sphere information. Here, we employ the length of the arc $\overset{\frown}{OS}$ and the direction to locate the spatial position, which are calculated according to

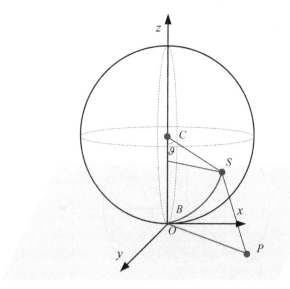

Figure 3.8 Illustration of the depth bounding sphere point projection onto the XOY plane.

$$\vartheta = \cos^{-1}\left(\frac{r - z_{\mathrm{s}}}{r}\right),\tag{3.4}$$

$$l = \pi \times \vartheta,\tag{3.5}$$

where r is the radius of the sphere, and l is the length of the arc $\overset{\frown}{OS}$.

The projection point $P(x_{\mathrm{p}}, y_{\mathrm{p}}, z_{\mathrm{p}})$ defines the position at a distance $\overset{\frown}{OS}$ from the centroid, where P is computed by

$$\begin{cases} x_{\mathrm{p}}^2 + y_{\mathrm{p}}^2 = l^2 \\ \frac{x_{\mathrm{p}}}{x_{\mathrm{s}}} = \frac{y_{\mathrm{p}}}{y_{\mathrm{s}}} \end{cases}.\tag{3.6}$$

We can accordingly obtain circular regions with radii of πr for the 3-D model description. Because there might be multiple attribute values at the surface point of the bounding sphere, it is possible that many pixels in the projection region have more than one attribute value. With these values for multiple layers in hand, we can obtain a group of SSCD images. Figure 3.9 shows some SSCD examples.

The main advantage of SSCD over other methods is that it is conformal and invariant to 3-D model rotations and scaling. The attribute values of the SSCD images can represent the spatial information of the 3-D model, which can preserve the global spatial structure.

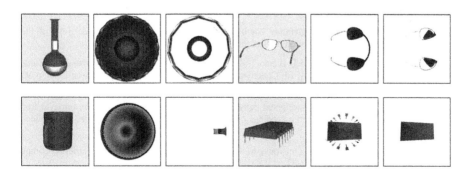

Figure 3.9 SSCD examples of four 3-D models.

3.5 SUMMARY

In this chapter, we introduce view extraction methods for view-based 3-D object description. The state-of-the-art methods can be divided into three categories: dense sampling viewpoints, predefined camera arrays, and generated views, which are detailed and discussed separately here. The main challenge of view extraction lies in the balance between sufficient data and redundancy. The merit of the dense sampling viewpoints methods is the coverage of information. However, rich information also brings about redundancy. The predefined camera array methods and generated view methods can reduce this redundancy, while the selected camera array may lose some information about the object.

REFERENCES

[1] Shih JL, Lee CH, Wang JT. A new 3D model retrieval approach based on the elevation descriptor. Pattern Recogn 2007;40(1):283-95.

[2] Ansary TF, Daoudi M, Vandeborre JP. A Bayesian 3D search engine using adaptive views clustering. IEEE Trans Multimed 2007;9(1):78-88.

[3] Daras P, Axenopoulos A. A 3D shape retrieval framework supporting multimodal queries. Int J Comput Vis 2010;89(2):229-47.

[4] Papadakis P, Pratikakis I, Theoharis T, Perantonis S. PANORAMA: a 3D shape descriptor based on panoramic views for unsupervised 3D object retrieval. Int J Comput Vis 2010;89(2):177-92.

[5] Gao Y, Dai QH, Zhang NY. 3D model comparison using spatial structure circular descriptor. Pattern Recogn 2010;43(3):1142-51.

[6] Tarik Filali A, Vandeborre JP, Daoudi M. Bayesian approach for 3D models retrieval based on characteristic views. In: Proceedings of the 17th International Conference on Pattern Recognition; 2004.

[7] Tarik Filali A, Vandeborre JP, Mahmoudi S, Daoudi M. A Bayesian framework for 3D models retrieval based on characteristic views. In: Proceedings of 2nd International Symposium on 3D Data Processing, Visualization and Transmission; 2004. p. 139-46.

[8] Furuya T, Ohbuchi R. Dense sampling and fast encoding for 3D model retrieval using bag-of-visual features. In: Proceedings of the ACM International Conference on Image and Video Retrieval; 2009.

[9] Ohbuchi R, Furuya T. Accelerating bag-of-features sift algorithm for 3D model retrieval. In: Proceedings of SAMT Workshop on Semantic 3D Media; 2008.

[10] Ohbuchi R, Osada K, Furuya T, Banno T. Salient local visual features for shape based 3D model retrieval. In: Proceedings of IEEE Conference on Shape Modeling and Applications; 2008. p. 93-102.

[11] Ohbuchi R, Furuya T. Scale-weighted dense bag of visual features for 3D model retrieval from a partial view 3D model. In: Proceedings of IEEE ICCV Workshop on Search in 3D and Video; 2009.

[12] Chen DY, Tian XP, Shen YT, Ouhyoung M. On visual similarity based 3D model retrieval. Comput Graph Forum 2003;22(3):223-32.

[13] Gao Y, Tang J, Li H, Dai Q, Zhang N. View-based 3D model retrieval with probabilistic graph model. Neurocomputing 2010;73(10-12):1900-5.

CHAPTER 4

View Selection

4.1 INTRODUCTION

As introduced in the previous chapter, the dense sampling viewpoints methods [1, 2] can provide rich information while also introducing redundant data. The predefined camera array methods [3, 4] and the generated view methods [5, 6] do not suffer from this problem. Therefore, view selection is critical to collect a compact set of views for 3-D object description.

View selection can be briefly illustrated as follows. *Given a group of initial views, select a small set of representative views for 3-D object representation.* For example, given a group of 200 initial views from different directions, the objective of view selection is to further select 10 or 20 representative views, which are discriminative to the 3-D object and also compact.

A fundamental problem is how to define the representative ability of views. Existing methods can be divided into two categories. The first category begins with multiple views of one object and determines a small group of views that reflect the 3-D object as much as possible. This type of methods which does not involve other information (just the 3-D object itself), is regarded as unsupervised methods. One typical unsupervised view selection process conducts view clustering first based on initial views and then selects one or more views from each view cluster. The merit of unsupervised methods is their simplicity and the fact that the data coverage is sufficient.

We note that the unsupervised methods neglect the discriminative objective of view selection, which is an important issue for a retrieval task. We propose an interactive view selection method in [7], which employs user relevance feedback information to discriminatively select views. The first priority of this method when selecting views is to isolate discriminatory properties. The initial views are first grouped into view clusters and the centroids become the candidate views for selection. A random walk process is conducted to determine the first representative view that is significantly related to other candidate views. This view is used in the 3-D object retrieval procedure and the top results are shown to the users for confirmation. The relevance feedback information is employed to select the next representative view based on the samples labeled as being relevant and irrelevant. For the newly selected view, an optimal distance metric is learned based on the labeled samples. All selected views are optimally combined for the next round search. In this framework, the representative views are incrementally selected in an interactive manner.

In this chapter, we will first introduce the unsupervised view selection methods, such as AVC [1]. Next, we introduce the interactive view selection method [7].

4.2 UNSUPERVISED VIEW SELECTION

The objective of unsupervised view selection methods is to select a group of compact views to characterize the 3-D object; these views should be able to show information that is as complete as possible. The informative views should be preserved for 3-D object representation. In these methods, no supervised information, such as annotation, is required. A typical procedure for unsupervised view selection methods is conducting view clustering to generate view clusters. An example is the AVC method [1].

In AVC, 320 initial views are captured, and the selection of characteristic views from these 320 initial views is formulated as a clustering task. A direct way is to conduct K-means [8], which is a traditional clustering method. However, this method is limited by the determined number of generated clusters. We note that the optimal numbers of representative views for different 3-D objects may vary significantly. Simple objects may require only a few characteristic views while complex objects may require more. Therefore, it is difficult to determine a fixed number of views for all 3-D objects. The representative view generation procedure should be flexible for different types of 3-D objects.

To overcome the limitation of K-means, the X-means [9] method is used for multiple view clustering in AVC. This method can select the optimal number of clusters from a range. Figure 4.1 shows the procedure for the AVC view clustering method. As shown in Figure 4.1, the number of view clusters starts from 1 and increases to the maximal number, that is, 40 in [1].

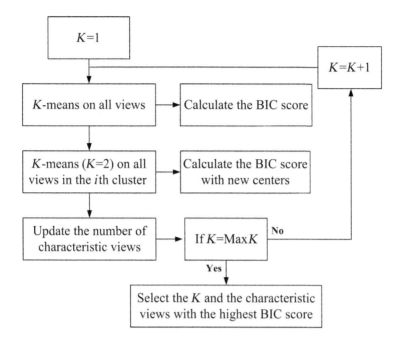

Figure 4.1 Illustration of the multiple view clustering procedure for characteristic view selection using AVC.

In each round, the K-means clustering method is conducted on all the views and the existing characteristic views are employed as the start centers. For each view cluster, the K-means method with $K=2$ is conducted and two new view clusters are generated. The Bayesian Information Criteria (BIC) [10] are employed here as the evaluation criteria to determine whether the clustering result is acceptable, that is, able to measure the representation model for the data based on the clustering results. The BIC scores of the original characteristic view and the two newly extracted views are calculated and the result with the higher BIC score is employed as the selected characteristic view. This procedure ends when either the maximal number of characteristic views is reached or the number of characteristic views no longer changes. Then, the overall BIC scores for each clustering results with different K can be calculated and the K with the highest overall BIC score is selected as the final result.

In this method, the BIC is regarded as the measure that evaluates the representative data selection. Given a representation model M_i with an ith view cluster V_i, the BIC score is measured by

$$\mathrm{BIC}(M_i) = \widehat{l}_i(V_i) - \frac{P_i}{2} \log N, \tag{4.1}$$

where P_i is the number of parameters in M_i, $\widehat{l}_i(V_i)$ is the maximal log-likelihood of M_i for the data, and N is the number of views for the cluster.

Here, the maximal likelihood estimate is calculated according to

$$\widehat{\theta}^2 = \frac{1}{N-K} \sum_i \left(d(v_i, v_{c_i})^2\right), \tag{4.2}$$

where $d(v_i, v_{c_i})$ is the distance between view v_i and the centroid view of the ith view cluster. In AVC, the 49-D Zernike moment [11] is employed as the feature for each view. Then, the log-likelihood of this view cluster is calculated according to

$$\widehat{l}_i(V_i) = \sum_j \left(\frac{1}{\sqrt{2\pi\widehat{\theta}}^{49}} - \frac{1}{2\widehat{\theta}^2} \|d(V_j, V_{c_i})\|^2 + \log \frac{N_i}{N} \right). \tag{4.3}$$

Following the AVC procedure, any group of multiple views generated by dense sampling viewpoints can obtain a small set of representative views. These views can be informative for 3-D objects with different number of views.

4.3 INTERACTIVE VIEW SELECTION

Unsupervised view selection methods target a group of views that can preserve the 3-D object information as completely as possible, while not taking into consideration the discriminatory information of the 3-D object. We note that the complete view may not only incur a high computational cost but may also degrade the retrieval performance due to mismatch of unimportant views. Additional characteristic views will increase the computing time of 3DOR.

Another key issue is that the discriminatory property is more important than the informative property in a 3DOR task; this case also holds true in other multimedia information retrieval tasks. Exploring the discriminatory views from a pool of views is an urgent but challenging task. We accordingly propose an interactive view selection method in [7], where the relevance feedback information is involved in the processing. Relevance feedback [12] has been investigated in multimedia information retrieval in recent decades and can improve retrieval performance via user interactions. Relevance feedback has also been employed in 3DOR [13]. User relevance feedback can enable explorations of the discriminatory information pertaining to a 3-D object. We have investigated the relevance feedback strategy and propose an interactive view selection framework, characterized by query view selection in [7]. This method can be briefly summarized as follows. Given a 3-D object with multiple views, view clustering is first conducted to group all the views into clusters. Then, the centroids of these clusters are selected as the candidate views for the object, which is similar to unsupervised view selection methods. The number of views can be reduced significantly from hundreds to tens. In these candidate views, a random walk process is conducted to generate the relevance among all these views and one initial representative view is selected for 3DOR. The user is required to label the top returned results as either relevant or irrelevant; this information is employed to select a new representative view from the pool of views. A distance metric is also determined for the new selected representative view associated with a combination weight. Then, all selected representative views are employed in the following 3DOR process. This methodology is repeated until satisfactory 3DOR results are obtained. Figure 4.2 illustrates the framework of the interactive query view selection method. The details of this work are introduced here, including multiview 3-D object matching, view clustering, initial query view selection, interactive view selection, the determination of a distance metric, and the linear combination of multiple query views.

4.3.1 Multiview 3-D Object Matching

Here, we first define the multiview distance measure between two 3-D objects, in which the minimal distance between two groups of views is employed. We denote the query object by Q and another object by O_i, respectively. The distance between the two objects, $d(Q, O_i,)$ is calculated according to

$$d(Q, O_i) = \sum_{j=1}^{K} \rho_j d(\widetilde{\mathbf{q}}_j, O_i),\qquad(4.4)$$

where K is the number of representative views for Q in the current 3DOR task, ρ_j is the weight for the ith representative view $\widetilde{\mathbf{q}}_j$, and $d(\widetilde{\mathbf{q}}_j, O_i)$ is defined as the minimal distance between $\widetilde{\mathbf{q}}_j$, O_i and all views in O_i, which is calculated according to

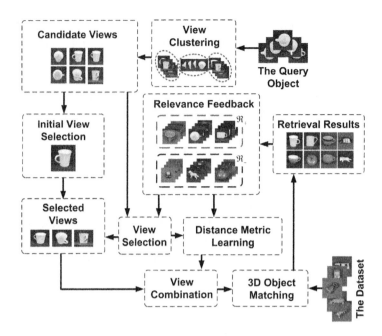

Figure 4.2 Illustration of the framework of the interactive query view selection [7].

$$d\left(\widetilde{\mathbf{q}}_j, O_i\right) = \min_p d\left(\widetilde{\mathbf{q}}_j, \mathbf{v}_{i,p}\right), \qquad (4.5)$$

where $\widetilde{\mathbf{q}}$ is the ith selected representative view of Q, and $\mathbf{v}_{i,p}$ is the pth view of O_i.

To measure the distance between two views, the Zernike moments [11, 14] are used here as the view feature. The Zernike moments are robust to image translation, scaling, and rotation and have been employed in many 3DOR tasks [1, 15]. Next, the distance $d\left(\widetilde{\mathbf{q}}_j, \mathbf{v}_{i,p}\right)$ is calculated according to

$$d\left(\widetilde{\mathbf{q}}_j, \mathbf{v}_{i,p}\right) = \left(\widetilde{\mathbf{q}}_j - \mathbf{v}_{i,p}\right)^T \mathbf{W}_j \left(\widetilde{\mathbf{q}}_j - \mathbf{v}_{i,p}\right), \qquad (4.6)$$

where $\mathbf{W}_j$ is the distance metric of the Mahalanobis distance for $\widetilde{\mathbf{q}}_j$. When no relevance feedback information is available, that is, during the first round of retrieval, $\mathbf{W}_j$ is initialized using the identity matrix $\mathbf{I}$, and $\rho_1 = 1$. With the user relevance feedback, $\mathbf{W}_j$ can be learned for the new representative view $\widetilde{\mathbf{q}}_j$ with a corresponding weight ρ_j. According to the above definition, each representative view of Q can find a best matched view from the views of O_i and the distances of these representative views can be linearly combined. 3DOR uses the distances of the objects in the data set to the query object Q.

4.3.2 View Clustering

To select the representative views, we first conduct a procedure similar to the unsupervised view selection method, that is, view clustering. For the query object, the views are grouped into clusters. Given a group of views $Q = \{\mathbf{q}_1, \ldots, \mathbf{q}_m\}$, the views are clustered into view groups, which can reduce the number of views for further processing. We employ the hierarchical agglomerative clustering (HAC) method [16]. HAC can group similar views into the same cluster until the intracluster distance exceeds a predefined threshold. Here, the Zernike moments are used as the feature of views. The HAC threshold is set as $10 \times \bar{d}$, where $\bar{d}$ is the mean distance between all view pairs. Generally, 10–30 clusters can be generated from each 3-D object. In each view cluster, the centroid view, which is close to all other views in the same cluster, is selected as one candidate view for Q. All these selected views compose a pool of candidate views.

4.3.3 Initial Query View Selection

With the pool of candidate views $\tilde{Q}$, we select the first representative view without any relevance feedback information: the first selected view should be informative for the 3-D object. The relationship among these candidate views can be accordingly explored.

We begin by formulating these views in a graph structure and using the random walk process to estimate the relevance. The random walk [17–19] can explore the relationship among a group of samples. Figure 4.3 illustrates the initial query view selection process.

For each candidate view, an initial score $\tau_i^{(0)}$ is determined according to the size of the corresponding view cluster. $\tau_i^{(0)}$ of the ith candidate view is calculated according to

$$\tau_i^{(0)} = \frac{|C(i)|}{\sum |C(j)|} \quad (j = 1, 2, \ldots, r), \tag{4.7}$$

where $|C(i)|$ is the number of the views in the ith view cluster.

A candidate view graph G is accordingly constructed from these candidate views. In G, each candidate view is denoted by one vertex $\mathbf{v}$ and the edge between each pair of vertices $\mathbf{v}_i$ and $\mathbf{v}_j$ is defined using the similarity s_{ij} between the two corresponding candidate views $\mathbf{v}_i$ and $\mathbf{v}_j$, which is calculated according to

$$s_{ij} = \exp\left(-\frac{d\left(\mathbf{v}_i, \mathbf{v}_j\right)}{\sigma}\right), \tag{4.8}$$

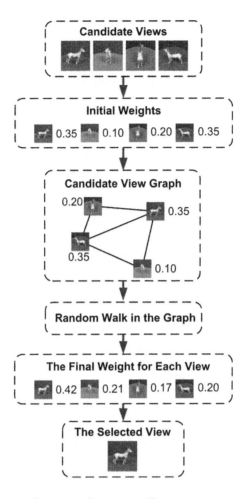

Figure 4.3 Illustration of the initial query view selection process [7].

where $d\left(\mathbf{v}_i, \mathbf{v}_j\right)$ is the distance between $\mathbf{v}_i$ and $\mathbf{v}_j$, and σ is a parameter.

We conduct a random walk process with the candidate view graph. Following the random walk process, the transition probability between two vertices $\mathbf{v}_i$ and $\mathbf{v}_j$ is calculated according to

$$p_{ij} = \frac{s_{ij}}{\sum_{k \neq i} s_{ik}} \tag{4.9}$$

and the random walk process is conducted according to

$$\tau_i^{(t+1)} = \alpha \sum_{k \neq i} \tau_k^{(t)} p_{ik} + (1 - \alpha) \tau_i^{(0)}, \tag{4.10}$$

where α is a parameter set to 0.5.

This process is repeated until convergence is achieved, when the final weights for each view are determined. The view from the pool with the highest score is selected as the initial query view, which will be used as the first query view for 3DOR with the multiview matching method introduced before.

4.3.4 Interactive View Selection with User Relevance Feedback

While 3DOR can be conducted using the initial query view, the results may not be satisfactory because only one view is employed in the retrieval process. To further improve the performance, the top-ranked results retrieved are shown to the user. If the user is satisfied with the results, the retrieval process is completed. However, if the results are not satisfactory to the user, an interactive view selection is started, where the user is required to manually label the highly ranked retrieved results as either relevant or irrelevant. If all top shown results have been manually annotated, several following results that have not been labeled by the user are provided for annotation.

Here, we denote the top returned results by $\Re$ and we let $\Re_+ = \{O_{1+}, O_{2+}, \ldots, O_{n_++}\}$ and $\Re_- = \{O_{1-}, O_{2-}, \ldots, O_{n_--}\}$ denote the set of 3-D objects labeled as relevant and irrelevant, respectively.

Let us assume the current retrieval round is $K - 1$ and that $\{\widetilde{\mathbf{q}}_l\ (l = 1, 2, \ldots, K - 1)\}$ denotes the selected $(K - 1)$ query views from the query object Q.

We aim to select the most discriminative view from the pool of remaining candidate views. In these circumstances, the required characteristic view should satisfy the following criterion:

- The selected view should be similar to the relevant samples and different from the irrelevant samples, which can increase the ability of the query object to be discriminative.

With this criterion, we then try to determine the view that can maximize the distance to irrelevant objects and minimize the distance to relevant objects. The objective function can be written as

$$\min_{\widetilde{\mathbf{q}}_K \in \{\widetilde{Q}/\widetilde{\mathbf{q}}_l(l=1,2,\ldots,K-1)\}} \{d\,(\widetilde{\mathbf{q}}_K, \Re_+) - d\,(\widetilde{\mathbf{q}}_K, \Re_-)\}. \qquad (4.11)$$

In the above formulation, the distance $d\,(\widetilde{\mathbf{q}}_K, \Re_+)$ between one view $\widetilde{\mathbf{q}}_K$ from the pool of candidate views and $\Re_+$ is calculated according to

$$d\left(\widetilde{\mathbf{q}}_K, \mathfrak{R}_+\right) = \sum_{O \in \mathfrak{R}_+} d\left(\widetilde{\mathbf{q}}_K, O\right) = \sum_{O \in \mathfrak{R}_+} \min_{\mathbf{v}_j \in O} d\left(\widetilde{\mathbf{q}}_K, \mathbf{v}_j\right) \qquad (4.12)$$

and the distance $d\left(\widetilde{\mathbf{q}}_K, \mathfrak{R}_-\right)$ between one view $\widetilde{\mathbf{q}}_K$ from the pool of candidate views and $\mathfrak{R}_-$ is calculated according to

$$d\left(\widetilde{\mathbf{q}}_K, \mathfrak{R}_-\right) = \sum_{O \in \mathfrak{R}_-} d\left(\widetilde{\mathbf{q}}_K, O\right) = \sum_{O \in \mathfrak{R}_-} \min_{\mathbf{v}_j \in O} d\left(\widetilde{\mathbf{q}}_K, \mathbf{v}_j\right). \qquad (4.13)$$

For each candidate view in the pool, we calculate $d\left(\widetilde{\mathbf{q}}_K, \mathfrak{R}_+\right) - d\left(\widetilde{\mathbf{q}}_K, \mathfrak{R}_-\right)$. Then the candidate view with the minimal value is selected as the Kth representative view of the query object. Distinct from the objective of unsupervised methods that preserve the complete information of the query object, this method can extract the discriminative information of the query object, which is the goal of the 3DOR task. One advantage of this method is that it does not aim to select all views, but rather just a small set of views that can represent the query object.

4.3.5 Learning a Distance Metric

Although the selected $\widetilde{q}_K$ is discriminatory with respect to the labeled samples, we can furthermore determine a distance metric for the new query view to enhance our ability to discriminate the query object. We follow the objective function for query view selection introduced above and employ the distance learning method introduced by Rui and Huang [12]. The objective of our methodology is to minimize the distance between the characteristic view and the relevant samples and to maximize the distance between the characteristic view and the irrelevant samples:

$$l \min \left\{ \sum_{O \in \mathfrak{R}_+} d\left(\widetilde{\mathbf{q}}_K, O\right) - \sum_{O \in \mathfrak{R}_-} d\left(\widetilde{\mathbf{q}}_K, O\right) \right\}$$

$$= \min \left\{ \sum_{i=1}^{n_+} d\left(\widetilde{\mathbf{q}}_K, \mathbf{v}_{i+}\right) - \sum_{i=1}^{n_-} d\left(\widetilde{\mathbf{q}}_K, \mathbf{v}_{i-}\right) \right\}, \qquad (4.14)$$

where $\mathbf{v}_{i+}$ is the view of the ith object in $\mathfrak{R}_+$ with the minimal distance to $\widetilde{\mathbf{q}}_K$ and $\mathbf{v}_{i-}$ is the view of the ith object in $\mathfrak{R}_-$ with the minimal distance to $\widetilde{\mathbf{q}}_K$ using the initial distance metric, that is, $\mathbf{W}_K = \mathbf{I}_{49}$ for the Zernike moment feature, in which the feature dimension is $D = 49$.

To simplify notations, the distance matrix $\mathbf{W}_K$ to be determined for the Kth query view is replaced with $\mathbf{W}$. A constraint $\det(\mathbf{W}) = 1$ is introduced to ensure that the optimization problem is well posed.

The optimal problem can be rewritten using the Lagrange multiplier method with the following constraint:

$$L = \sum_{i=1}^{n_+} d\left(\widetilde{\mathbf{q}}_K, \mathbf{v}_{i+}\right) - \sum_{i=1}^{n_-} d\left(\widetilde{\mathbf{q}}_K, \mathbf{v}_{i-}\right) + \lambda\left(\det\left(\mathbf{W}\right) - 1\right). \quad (4.15)$$

We next tried to solve this optimization task. For the (s, t)th element of $\mathbf{W}$, i.e., w_{st}, we can achieve

$$\frac{\partial L}{\partial w_{st}} = \sum_{i=1}^{n_+} \frac{\partial d\left(\widetilde{\mathbf{q}}_K, \mathbf{v}_{i+}\right)}{\partial w_{st}} - \sum_{i=1}^{n_-} \frac{\partial d\left(\widetilde{\mathbf{q}}_K, \mathbf{v}_{i-}\right)}{\partial w_{st}}$$

$$+ \lambda(-1)^{s+t} \det\left(\overline{\mathbf{W}}_{st}\right), \quad (4.16)$$

where $\overline{\mathbf{W}}_{st}$ is the $(D-1) \times (D-1)$ matrix generated by removing the sth row and the tth column of $\mathbf{W}$.

$\sum_{i=1}^{n_+} \frac{\partial d(\widetilde{\mathbf{q}}_K, \mathbf{v}_{i+})}{\partial w_{st}}$ and $\sum_{i=1}^{n_-} \frac{\partial d(\widetilde{\mathbf{q}}_K, \mathbf{v}_{i-})}{\partial w_{st}}$ can be calculated according to

$$\sum_{i=1}^{n_+} \frac{\partial d\left(\widetilde{\mathbf{q}}_K, \mathbf{v}_{i+}\right)}{\partial w_{st}} = \sum_{i=1}^{n_+} \frac{\partial\left(\widetilde{\mathbf{q}}_K - \mathbf{v}_{i+}\right)^T \mathbf{W}\left(\widetilde{\mathbf{q}}_K - \mathbf{v}_{i+}\right)}{\partial w_{st}}$$

$$= \sum_{i=1}^{n_+} \left(\mathbf{v}_{i+}\left(s\right) - \widetilde{\mathbf{q}}_K\left(s\right)\right)\left(\mathbf{v}_{i+}\left(t\right) - \widetilde{\mathbf{q}}_K\left(t\right)\right) \quad (4.17)$$

and

$$\sum_{i=1}^{n_-} \frac{\partial d\left(\widetilde{\mathbf{q}}_K, \mathbf{v}_{i-}\right)}{\partial w_{st}} - \sum_{i=1}^{n_-} \frac{\partial\left(\widetilde{\mathbf{q}}_K - \mathbf{v}_{i-}\right)^T \mathbf{W}\left(\widetilde{\mathbf{q}}_K - \mathbf{v}_{i-}\right)}{\partial w_{st}}$$

$$= \sum_{i=1}^{n_-} \left(\mathbf{v}_{i-}\left(s\right) - \widetilde{\mathbf{q}}_K\left(s\right)\right)\left(\mathbf{v}_{i-}\left(t\right) - \widetilde{\mathbf{q}}_K\left(t\right)\right). \quad (4.18)$$

Letting $\frac{\partial L}{\partial w_{st}} = 0$, we can derive the following equation:

$$\det\left(\overline{\mathbf{W}}_{st}\right) = \frac{\sum_{i=1}^{n_-} \frac{\partial d\left(\widetilde{\mathbf{q}}_K, \mathbf{v}_{i-}\right)}{\partial w_{st}} - \sum_{i=1}^{n_+} \frac{\partial d\left(\widetilde{\mathbf{q}}_K, \mathbf{v}_{i+}\right)}{\partial w_{st}}}{\lambda(-1)^{s+t}}. \quad (4.19)$$

We let $\mathbf{W}^{-1} = [a_{st}]$, that is, a_{st} is the (s, t)th element of $\mathbf{W}^{-1}$.

We can rewrite a_{st} as

$$a_{st} = \frac{(-1)^{s+t} \det\left(\overline{\mathbf{W}}_{st}\right)}{\det(\mathbf{W})}$$

$$= (-1)^{s+t} \det\left(\overline{\mathbf{W}}_{st}\right)$$

$$= (-1)^{s+t} \frac{\sum_{i=1}^{n_-} \frac{\partial d\left(\widetilde{\mathbf{q}}_K, \mathbf{v}_{i-}\right)}{\partial w_{st}} - \sum_{i=1}^{n_+} \frac{\partial d\left(\widetilde{\mathbf{q}}_K, \mathbf{v}_{i+}\right)}{\partial w_{st}}}{\lambda(-1)^{s+t}}$$

$$= \frac{\sum_{i=1}^{n_-} \frac{\partial d\left(\widetilde{\mathbf{q}}_K, \mathbf{v}_{i-}\right)}{\partial w_{st}} - \sum_{i=1}^{n_+} \frac{\partial d\left(\widetilde{\mathbf{q}}_K, \mathbf{v}_{i+}\right)}{\partial w_{st}}}{\lambda}. \tag{4.20}$$

Letting $\mathbf{C} = [c_{st}]$, we obtain

$$c_{st} = \sum_{i=1}^{n_-} \frac{\partial d\left(\widetilde{\mathbf{q}}_K, \mathbf{v}_{i-}\right)}{\partial w_{st}} - \sum_{i=1}^{n_+} \frac{\partial d\left(\widetilde{\mathbf{q}}_K, \mathbf{v}_{i+}\right)}{\partial w_{st}}. \tag{4.21}$$

We then obtain that

$$\mathbf{C} = \lambda \mathbf{W}^{-1}. \tag{4.22}$$

It can be derived that

$$\det(\mathbf{C}) = \lambda^D \det\left(\mathbf{W}^{-1}\right) = \lambda^D. \tag{4.23}$$

Therefore, we can obtain

$$\lambda = (\det(\mathbf{C}))^{\frac{1}{D}} \tag{4.24}$$

and

$$\mathbf{W} = \lambda \mathbf{C}^{-1} = (\det(\mathbf{C}))^{\frac{1}{D}} \mathbf{C}^{-1}. \tag{4.25}$$

The learned distance metric $\mathbf{W}$ for the Kth query view can be used in the following retrieval rounds.

4.3.6 Multiple Query Views Linear Combination

With the K selected query views, the next round of 3DOR is based on a combination of these views. We note that different query views may have different effects on the description of the object. Therefore, we aim to linearly combine these query views with different weights instead of simply adding them with equal weights.

The following objective function is introduced to determine the weights of the multiple-view linear combination:

$$
\min f(\rho) = \min \left\{ \sum_{i=1}^{K} \sum_{O \in \mathfrak{R}_+} \rho_i d\left(\tilde{\mathbf{q}}_i, O\right) - \sum_{i=1}^{K} \sum_{O \in \mathfrak{R}_-} \rho_i d\left(\tilde{\mathbf{q}}_i, O\right) \right.
$$

$$
\left. + \gamma \sum_{i=1}^{K} \|\rho_i\|^2 \right\}
$$

$$
s.t. \quad \sum_{i=1}^{K} \rho_i = 1. \tag{4.26}
$$

This objective function contains two components: a loss term and a l2-norm regularizer term related to the weights. The first term is the summation of the weighted distances between the selected query view and all the relevant objects. The second term is a l2-norm regularizer that is the average prior to the weights, that is, the weights should tend toward being identical given a lack of other information.

The optimization task is solved by using the Lagrangian method, and the objective function becomes

$$
\min \left\{ \sum_{i=1}^{K} \sum_{O \in \mathfrak{R}_+} \rho_i d\left(\tilde{\mathbf{q}}_i, O\right) - \sum_{i=1}^{K} \sum_{O \in \mathfrak{R}_-} \rho_i d\left(\tilde{\mathbf{q}}_i, O\right) \right.
$$

$$
\left. + \gamma \|\rho\|^2 + \eta \left(\sum_{i=1}^{K} \rho_i - 1 \right) \right\}. \tag{4.27}
$$

It can be derived that

$$
\rho_j = \frac{1}{K} + \frac{\sum_{i=1}^{K} \sum_{O \in \mathfrak{R}_+} d\left(\tilde{\mathbf{q}}_i, O\right) - \sum_{i=1}^{K} \sum_{O \in \mathfrak{R}_-} d\left(\tilde{\mathbf{q}}_i, O\right)}{2K\gamma}
$$

$$
- \frac{\sum_{O \in \mathfrak{R}_+} d\left(\tilde{\mathbf{q}}_j, O\right) - \sum_{O \in \mathfrak{R}_-} d\left(\tilde{\mathbf{q}}_j, O\right)}{2\gamma}, \tag{4.28}
$$

where γ is empirically set to be $K \max_{O \in \mathfrak{R}_+} d\left(\tilde{\mathbf{q}}_K, O\right)$. This value guarantees that all weights are nonnegative.

4.3.7 The Computational Cost

In the above framework, the computational cost for each round of interactive view selection is $O\left((n_+ + n_-)D^2 n_v^2\right)$. Here, D is the dimension of the employed feature, which is 49 for the employed Zernike moment feature, n_v is the average number of views for each object, K is the number of selected query views, and n_+ and n_- are the numbers of labeled relevant and irrelevant objects, respectively. The computational cost of the distance metric learning scales as $O\left((n_+ + n_-)D^3\right)$. In the multiple-view combination step, the learning cost after the Kth relevance feedback is $O\left((n_+ + n_-)D^2 n_v^2 + (n_+ + n_-)D^3\right) + O\left(n_o D^2 n_v\right)$, where n_o is the number of 3-D objects in the database. In this part, the first component derives from the learning step and the second component comes from the object matching. As for each retrieval round, the distance metric learning process is conducted for the new selected query view only. As a result, the overall computational cost is low.

4.4 SUMMARY

In this chapter, we reviewed and discussed the view selection methods in V3DOR, including unsupervised view selection methods and interactive view selection methods. The targets for view selection of these two types of methods are different. In unsupervised view selection methods, the objective is to preserve the complete information about the 3-D object. On the other hand, for the interactive view selection method, the goal is to select the most discriminatory views. In comparison with the predefined camera array view extraction methods, which perform the view selection in the camera array setting procedure, the unsupervised view selection methods are more robust when dealing with different types of 3-D objects. The selected views are not limited to specific directions of a fixed camera array, which result in a more flexible technique for handling different circumstances.

The discriminatory information used for a 3DOR task is much more important than the complete data, which makes the interactive method preferable. On the other hand, the discriminative information from the interactive view selection method has a high associated computational cost. The user relevance feedback apparently requires additional human labor in the retrieval process, which limits real-time 3DOR on some scales.

Selecting a group of discriminatory views in a pool of views is still a challenging task in V3DOR. There is a trade-off between discriminatory information and computational cost. A possible solution is to involve large-scale, predefined 3-D object semantics, which can provide semi-supervised information for view selection given a group of views for one 3-D object. The view-capturing background and the context information can be used for view selection with priors, which can be determined from the existing data.

REFERENCES

[1] Ansary TF, Daoudi M, Vandeborre JP. A Bayesian 3D search engine using adaptive views clustering. IEEE Trans Multimed 2007;9(1):78-88.

[2] Ohbuchi R, Osada K, Furuya T, Banno T. Salient local visual features for shape based 3D model retrieval. In: Proceedings of IEEE Conference on Shape Modeling and Applications; 2008. p. 93-102.

[3] Shih JL, Lee CH, Wang JT. A new 3D model retrieval approach based on the elevation descriptor. Pattern Recogn 2007;40(1):283-95.

[4] Daras P, Axenopoulos A. A 3D shape retrieval framework supporting multimodal queries. Int J Comput Vis 2010;89(2):229-47.

[5] Papadakis P, Pratikakis I, Theoharis T, Perantonis S. PANORAMA: a 3D shape descriptor based on panoramic views for unsupervised 3D object retrieval. Int J Comput Vis 2010;89(2):177-92.

[6] Gao Y, Dai QH, Zhang NY. 3D model comparison using spatial structure circular descriptor. Pattern Recogn 2010;43(3):1142-51.

[7] Gao Y, Wang M, Zha Z, Tian Q, Dai Q, Zhang N. Less is more: efficient 3D object retrieval with query view selection. IEEE Trans Multimed 2011;11(5):1007-18.

[8] Duda RO, Hart PE. Pattern classification and scene analysis. New York: Wiley; 1973.

[9] Pelleg D, Moore A. X-means: extending K-means with efficient estimation of the number of clusters. In: International Conference on Machine Learning; 2000. p. 727-34.

[10] Schwarz G. Estimating the dimension of a model. Ann Statist 1978;6:461-4.

[11] Kim WY, Kim YS. A region-based shape descriptor using Zernike moments. Signal Process Image Commun 2000;16(1-2):95-102.

[12] Rui Y, Huang T. Optimizing learning in image retrieval. In: Proceedings of the IEEE Conference on Computer Vision and Pattern Recognition; 2000. p. 1236-43.

[13] Akbar S, Kung J, Wagner R, Prihatmanto A. Multi-feature integration with relevance feedback on 3D model similarity retrieval. In: Proceedings of the International Conference on Information Integration and Web-Based Applications Services; 2006. p. 77-86.

[14] Khotanzad A, Hong YH. Invariant image recognition by Zernike moments. IEEE Trans Pattern Anal Mach Intell 1990;12(5):489-97.

[15] Chen DY, Tian XP, Shen YT, Ouhyoung M. On visual similarity based 3D model retrieval. Comput Graph Forum 2003;22(4):223-32.

[16] Steinbach M, Karypis G, Kumar V. A comparison of document clustering techniques. In: Proceedings of KDD Workshop on Text Mining; 2000.

[17] Page L, Brin S, Motwani R, Winograd T. The page rank citation ranking: bringing order to the web. Stanford Digital Libraries Working Paper; 1998.

[18] Jing YS, Baluja S. Visual rank: applying page rank to large-scale image search. IEEE Trans Pattern Anal Mach Intell 2008;30(11):1877-90.

[19] Zhang ST, Yang M, Cour T, Yu K, Metaxas DN. Query specific rank fusion for image retrieval. IEEE Trans Pattern Anal Mach Intell 2014.

CHAPTER 5

View Representation

5.1 INTRODUCTION

Feature extraction is an integral part of multimedia information retrieval. The majority of previous methods are based on 3-D models [1], which can be divided into statistics [2, 3], extension-based descriptors, volume-based descriptors, and surface geometry descriptors.

Statistics describe the properties of 3-D models such as the number of vertices and polygons, the bounding sphere, and the statistical moment. One example of simple statistics is the bounding volume of the minimal bounding rectangular box for a 3-D model [2]. Other types of statistics include the geometry moment [4, 5] and the shape distribution [6–8]. Extension-based descriptors extract the sampled features along the spatial direction from the object center. Example extension-based descriptors include ray sampling with spherical harmonics [9, 10] and extensions for ray sampling [11, 12]. Volume-based descriptors measure the volumetric representations through the voxel grids of the object surface, such as the discretized model volume, the shape histogram [13], the voxelized volume [14–17], and so on. Surface geometry descriptors calculate the surface characteristics, such as the surface curvature [18, 19] and the extended Gaussian image [20].

View representation in V3DOR is composed of two primary issues: visual feature extraction and multiple-view weighting. For view feature extraction, several effective features have been introduced, such as Zernike moments [21] and Fourier descriptors [22]. In recent years, the bag-of-visual-features (BoVF) method has been investigated in V3DOR. Some studies [23–25] have focused on view feature extraction from the bag-of-words direction and how to accelerate the matching process [26]. Multiple-view weighting is another intriguing topic as different views may have different weights in the object representation, particularly in the 3DOR process. In the last part of this chapter, we introduce our work on multiple-view weight learning.

This chapter is organized as follows. We first introduce existing shape features that are widely used, including Zernike moments and Fourier descriptors. Next, we discuss the BoVF method and its extensions on V3DOR. We then introduce our work on determining the view weights [27]. A summary of this chapter is given at the end.

5.2 SHAPE FEATURE EXTRACTION

In this section, we introduce two widely used shape features: Zernike moments [28] and Fourier descriptors [22].

5.2.1 Zernike Moments

Moments are recognized as popular pattern representation methods in many applications [28, 29]. The moment feature can preserve the global information of images. A typical moment is defined by

$$m_{st} = \sum_x \sum_y x^s y^t f(x, y), \tag{5.1}$$

where m_{st} is the $(s + t)$th order moment of the image $f(x, y)$.

As introduced in Hu [28], several moments with nonlinear functions are invariant to image scaling, rotation, and translation. Zernike moments are a class of orthogonal comments and their rotational invariance is important for shape representation. A set of complex polynomials are used to calculate Zernike moments. These polynomials form an orthogonal set over the interior of the unit circle. These polynomials are denoted by $\{P_{st}(x, y)\}$, which are defined as

$$P_{st}(x, y) = P_{st}(\rho, \theta) = R_{st}(\rho) \exp(jt\theta), \tag{5.2}$$

where s is a positive integer or 0 and t are positive and negative integers subject to the constraints that $s - |t|$ is even and $|t|$ is no more than s. ρ is the length from the origin to (x, y) and θ is the angle between ρ and the x-axis. The radial polynomial is defined as

$$R_{st}(\rho) = \sum_{z=0}^{\frac{s-|t|}{2}} (-1)^z \frac{(s-z)!}{z! \left(\frac{s+|t|}{2} - z\right)! \left(\frac{s-|t|}{2} - z\right)!} \rho^{s-2z}. \tag{5.3}$$

Zernike moments are the projections of the image function onto the orthogonal basic functions. The $(s + t)$th Zernike moment for an image function $f(x, y)$ is defined as

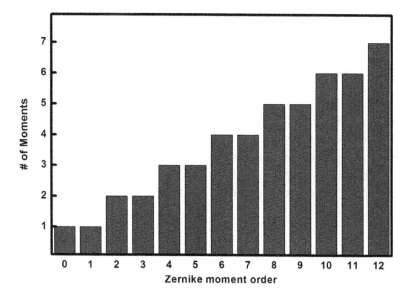

Figure 5.1 The numbers of Zernike moments for different moment orders.

$$ZM_{st} = \frac{s+1}{\pi} \sum_x \sum_y f(x,y) P_{st}(\rho, \theta).$$ (5.4)

For Zernike moments, the number of moments for the kth order is $\left(\frac{k}{2} + 1\right)(k + 1)$. The numbers of Zernike moments for different orders are shown in Figure 5.1.

Generally, the 49-D Zernike moments from order 0 to order 12 are employed for view features [30–32].

Another popular feature is Krawtchouk moments [33], which are another moment-based feature with Krawtchouk polynomials.

5.2.2 Fourier Descriptor

Discrete Fourier transform (DFT) [22] can convert a group of equally spaced samples of a signal function into a list of coefficients. These coefficients comprise a finite combination of complex sinusoids ordered by frequency. The sampled function is converted via DFT from time domain to frequency domain.

For a given signal $f_t(i,j)$, DFT can be calculated according to

$$\text{DFT}\,(k,m) = \sum_{i=0}^{N-1}\sum_{j=0}^{N-10} f_t\,(i,j)\exp\left(-\widehat{j}\left(\frac{2\pi\,ik}{N} + \frac{2\pi\,jm}{N}\right)\right). \qquad (5.5)$$

The magnitude of DFT is invariant to circular translations, which makes DFT a good candidate for shape description [30, 34, 35]. The first $K \times M$ harmonic amplitudes are employed as the Fourier descriptors for a shape. To accelerate the Fourier descriptor extraction procedure, the fast Fourier transform (FFT) can be employed to replace DFT.

5.3 THE BAG-OF-VISUAL-FEATURES METHOD

The BoVF method [36–38] has been widely employed in image and video retrieval tasks because of its superior ability to discriminate visual information. Recently, BoVF has been investigated in V3DOR [24, 25]. In this section, we first introduce the bag-of-visual-words methods in V3DOR, then provide the bag-of-region-words (BoRW) method.

5.3.1 The Bag-of-Visual-Words

In the bag-of-visual-words method, image features are regarded as words, following the path of the bag-of-words method in text processing. In document classification, the bag-of-words method counts the occurrence of each individual word. Similarly, a bag-of-visual-words method is a sparse counting vector of the occurrence of a visual vocabulary from local visual features.

Ohbuchi et al. [25] first introduce the bag-of-visual-words method in 3DOR. In this study, post-normalization of position and scale is conducted for all 3-D models. This technique aims to produce renderings of all 3-D models at an appropriate size. Then, the range images from N_i directions are rendered for each 3-D model. For each range image, the scale-invariant feature transform (SIFT) feature [39] is extracted and all local visual features are grouped into clusters to generate a visual codebook. This visual codebook is used to quantize all local visual features into visual words. A histogram of these visual words can be generated reflecting the distribution of visual words generated with N_v bins for the 3-D model description. The distance between two 3-D models is calculated using the

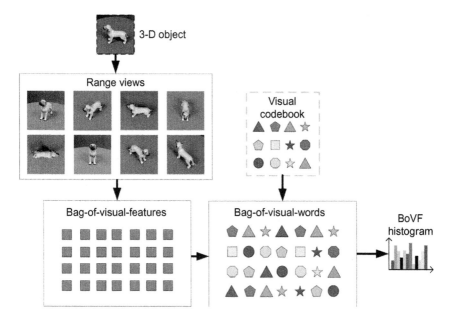

Figure 5.2 The framework for the BoVF-based 3DOR method in Ohbuchi et al. [25].

Kullback-Leibler divergence [40]. Figure 5.2 illustrates the framework of the study by Ohbuchi et al. in [25].

In a study by Furuya and Ohbuchi [24], the SIFT keypoint extraction process is replaced by feature point selection using dense sampling. For each range image, 300 points are densely sampled for the local SIFT feature extraction. Because the BoVF extraction is computationally expensive, Ohbuchi and Furuya [23] furthermore introduce a method to employ a graphics processing unit to accelerate the process in 3DOR. Other improvements proposed by these authors include a scale-weighted dense BoVF [26].

5.3.2 The Bag-of-Region-Words
The BoVF method focuses on the local feature level for feature points, while a more semantic description can be further explored to improve 3DOR performance. In this direction, we introduce a BoRW method in [41] for 3-D object description. The BoRW method, which is distinct from the traditional BoVF method, aims to represent region-level features rather than keypoint-level features. Figure 5.3 shows the framework of the BoRW method. This figure highlights the five steps of the BoRW feature extraction: BoVF extraction for each view, generation of a visual codebook,

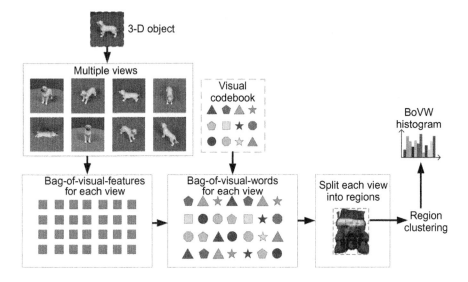

Figure 5.3 The framework for the BoRW method [25].

bag-of-visual-words generation for each view (feature quantization), image splitting, and image region clustering. The advantage of this method lies in its more complete semantic description compared with the BoVF method.

To generate a BoRW feature for a 3-D object given a group of views, the SIFT feature [39] is first extracted for each view $v_i \in \{v_1, v_2, \ldots, v_{n_v}\}$ with dense sampling. Generally, hundreds to thousands of uniformly distributed keypoints are densely sampled from each view. The 128-D SIFT feature is employed here.

A large number of features from a selected view set are employed to train a codebook with n_c words. With this codebook, each visual feature in each view can be encoded into one word of the codebook, following a nearest-neighbor technique. Then, each view can be represented by a bag-of-visual-words descriptor.

To further represent the region-level information of each 3-D object, these views are split into n_r regions with different sizes and a bag-of-visual-words descriptor is generated for each region. It is therefore possible to achieve a region-level 3-D object representation. Figure 5.4 illustrates an image splitting example. It is noted that only the simple image splitting methods are introduced here. Towards better performance, other methods, such as image segmentation or super-pixel extraction, can be applied.

Figure 5.4 Example image splitting method.

To describe the region information, each region is assigned a weight corresponding to its size. Generally, a larger region, which can reflect more information than a smaller region, should be given a higher weight. Thus, the weight for the ith region can be defined by

$$\omega_i = \frac{Area(i)}{Area(v)},\tag{5.6}$$

where $Area(i)$ is the area of the ith region, and $Area(v)$ is the area of the view.

Therefore, in total, there are $n_v \times n_r$ regions for one 3-D object O. By using the BoVF descriptor, all these image regions can be clustered into groups, where the hierarchical agglomerative clustering (HAC) method [42] can be used. One representative region is then selected from each region cluster. The representative region is also assigned a weight corresponding to the size of the cluster and the weights for all the regions in that cluster.

Let the kth cluster be $\{\psi_k^1, \psi_k^2, \ldots, \psi_k^t\}$, and the corresponding weight vector be $\{\omega_k^1, \omega_k^2, \ldots, \omega_k^t\}$, where t is the number of image regions in this cluster. The weight for the kth cluster w_k is calculated according to

$$w_k = \frac{\sum_i \omega_k^i}{\sum_{i,k} \omega_k^i}.\tag{5.7}$$

Here, we denote the BoVF descriptor for the representative region by f_k. Each 3-D object can be represented by a BoRW feature, that is, $\{\{f_1, w_1\}, \ldots, \{f_k, w_k\}\}$.

The pairwise object distance can be calculated for two 3-D objects using the BoRW features and many-to-many matching methods. One example is the earth mover's distance (EMD) [43]. The EMD-based distance between two BoRWs, BoRW$_1$ and BoRW$_2$, is defined as a minimization over all possible flows $F = [F_{ij}]$, subject to the following constrains:

$$\text{EMD}(\text{BoRW}_1, \text{BoRW}_2) = \min_F \left\{ \sum_{i=1}^{a} \sum_{j=1}^{b} d(f_i^1, f_j^2) F_{ij} \right\}, \qquad (5.8)$$

where

$$\forall 1 \leq i, j \leq a : F_{ij} \geq 0, \qquad (5.9)$$

$$\forall 1 \leq j \leq b : \sum_{j=1}^{b} F_{ij} = w_i^1 \qquad (5.10)$$

and

$$\forall 1 \leq i \leq a : \sum_{i=1}^{a} F_{ij} = w_j^2. \qquad (5.11)$$

V3DOR can accordingly be conducted given this BoRW pairwise distance for 3-D objects. The advantage of BoRW is that it can represent not only the global information of each 3-D object but also the part-based information of each 3-D object. However, BoRW is effective only when two similar 3-D objects are partially matched.

5.4 LEARNING THE WEIGHTS FOR MULTIPLE VIEWS

In V3DOR, weighting representative views is an important task because these views may play different roles in the retrieval process. Some views can be more discriminative than others for the query objects. Therefore, it is important to conduct not only a discriminative view selection procedure but also a weighting process. We have introduced a view weighting method in Chapter 4—an interactive query view selection method with view weighting. We note that this method requires user relevance feedback, which limits its utility. In this section, we introduce our work related to the multiple-view weighting task without any supervised information.

Without a loss of generality, we formulate V3DOR as a typical retrieval task with bag queries. The retrieval task with bag queries can be defined as follows:

Given a query Q with k components, that is, $Q = \{q_1, q_2, \ldots, q_k\}$, the distance between Q and another sample S is measured by

$$d(Q, S) = \sum_{i=1}^{k} w_i d(q_i, S), \qquad (5.12)$$

where w_i is the weight for q_i.

Given a bag of queries, the objective is to update the weighting for each query in the bag of Q without requiring additional human input. Here the pseudorelevant feedback information is employed for weight learning and a k-partite graph reinforcement model is introduced for information propagation [27]. The k-partite graph reinforcement model can optimize the weights of multiple components via an iterative process. All components are assigned a weight after this k-partite graph reinforcement procedure. In this part we first introduce the k-partite graph reinforcement model, and then apply it in the weight learning task of multiple views.

5.4.1 *K*-Partite Graph Reinforcement

Here, we first recall the definition of the k-partite graph [44] and introduce the k-partite graph reinforcement model.

A k-partite graph is a graph whose vertices can be partitioned into k disjoint sets.

Therefore, a k-partite graph is composed of k subsets of vertices, and the edges only exist between two vertices from two different subsets. Figure 5.5 shows an example of a k-partite graph. When k is reduced to 2, the k-partite graph is a bipartite graph. For clarity, we first define notations and definitions used here in Table 5.1.

First, the k-partite graph construction with a group of samples is introduced. Given k samples $\{S_1, S_2, \ldots, S_k\}$, each sample S_i includes n_i subsamples $\{\mathbf{S}_{i1}, \mathbf{S}_{i2}, \ldots, \mathbf{S}_{in_i}\}$. The k-partite graph G is constructed using $\{S_1, S_2, \ldots, S_k\}$, in which each partite denotes one sample, and each vertex in that partite denotes one subsample from the sample. $\mathbf{E}^{ij}$ is the $n_i \times n_j$ edge matrix between two partite in G, and $\mathbf{E}_{st}^{ij}$ denotes the relevance between the sth subsample of the ith sample and the tth subsample of the jth sample. The initial weight $\mathbf{g}_i^0$ is an $n_i \times 1$ initial weight vector for the ith sample, that is, the ith partite of G.

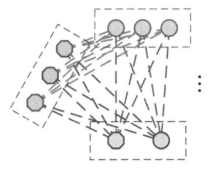

Figure 5.5 Example of a k-partite graph.

Table 5.1 Notations and definitions relevant to the *k*-partite graph reinforcement model	
Notation	**Definition**
S_i	The ith sample with n_i subsamples.
S_{ij}	The jth subsample of S_i.
G	The k-partite graph.
$\mathbf{g}_i$	The weight vector for the ith partite of G, which is $n_i \times 1$.
$\mathbf{g}_i^0$	The initial weight vector for the ith partite of G, which is $n_i \times 1$.
$\mathbf{g}_i^n$	The weight vector for the ith partite of G after n round reinforcement process, which is $n_i \times 1$.
$\mathbf{E}^{ij}$	The edge matrix between the ith partite and the jth partite of G, which is $n_i \times n_j$.
$\mathbf{L}^{ij}$	The transition matrix from the ith partite and the jth partite of G, which is $n_i \times n_j$.
$\mathbf{D}^{ij}$	The diagonal matrix generated from $\mathbf{E}^{st}$, which is $n_i \times n_j$.
α	The weighting parameter in the k-partite graph reinforcement process.

After constructing the k-partite graph G, the objective is to optimize the weights among all these k-partites. When two partites are close they have a high possibility of sharing similar weights for object representation. Eq. (5.13) provides the objective function of the k-partite graph reinforcement process. Here, $\mathbf{L}^{ij}$ is the $n_i \times n_j$ transition matrix between the ith partite and the jth partite and α_i are the weights in the reinforcement process, where $\alpha_i \in (0, 1]$.

$$\begin{cases} \mathbf{g}_1^{n+1} = \alpha_1 \times \mathbf{g}_1^0 + (1 - \alpha_1) \times \frac{1}{\kappa - 1} \sum_{i \neq 1} \mathbf{L}^{i1} \mathbf{g}_i^n \\ \mathbf{g}_2^{n+1} = \alpha_2 \times \mathbf{g}_2^0 + (1 - \alpha_2) \times \frac{1}{\kappa - 1} \sum_{i \neq 2} \mathbf{L}^{i2} \mathbf{g}_i^n \\ \vdots \\ \mathbf{g}_k^{n+1} = \alpha_k \times \mathbf{g}_k^0 + (1 - \alpha_k) \times \frac{1}{k - 1} \sum_{i \neq k} \mathbf{L}^{ik} \mathbf{g}_i^n \end{cases}, \qquad (5.13)$$

where the transition matrix $\mathbf{L}^{ij}$ is generated by:

$$\mathbf{L}^{ij} = \mathbf{D}_r^{ij-1} \mathbf{E}^{ij} \qquad (5.14)$$

and

$$\mathbf{D}_r^{ij}(a, a) = \sum_b e_{ab}^{ij}. \qquad (5.15)$$

Based on this iteration process, the weights of all vertices in G can be updated. Because convergence is an important issue, the convergence of the iterative process in Eq. (5.13) is provided here.

Two matrix-related lemmas are first introduced here.

Lemma 1. *For any matrix* $\mathbf{A} \in C^{n \times n}$ *and matrix norm* $\|\bullet\|$ *defined on* $C^{n \times n}$, *we have* $\rho(\mathbf{A}) \leq \|\mathbf{A}\|$. *Here,* $\rho(\mathbf{A})$ *is the spectral radius of matrix* $\mathbf{A}$.

Lemma 2. *For any matrix* $\mathbf{A} \in C^{n \times n}$ *with* $\rho(\mathbf{A}) < 1$, *we have* $\lim_{t \to \infty} \mathbf{A}^t = 0$.

For the ith partite of G, we can calculate a difference function between $\mathbf{g}_i^{n+1}$ and $\mathbf{g}_i^n$ according to

$$\mathbf{g}_i^{n+1} - \mathbf{g}_i^n = \frac{1-\alpha_i}{K-1} \sum_{j \neq i} \mathbf{L}^{ij} \left(\mathbf{g}_i^n - \mathbf{g}_i^{n-1} \right), \qquad (5.16)$$

where $i = 1, 2, \ldots, k$.

With these difference functions, we can furthermore define

$$\mathbf{G}^{n+1} = \left(\mathbf{g}_1^{n+1} - \mathbf{g}_1^n, \mathbf{g}_2^{n+1} - \mathbf{g}_2^n, \ldots, \mathbf{g}_i^{n+1} - \mathbf{g}_i^n, \ldots, \mathbf{g}_k^{n+1} - \mathbf{g}_k^n \right)$$

$$= \left(\mathbf{g}_1^n - \mathbf{g}_1^{n-1}, \mathbf{g}_2^n - \mathbf{g}_2^{n-1}, \ldots, \mathbf{g}_i^n - \mathbf{g}_i^{n-1}, \ldots, \mathbf{g}_k^n - \mathbf{g}_k^{n-1} \right)$$

$$\times \begin{bmatrix} 0 & \frac{1-\alpha_2}{k-1}\mathbf{L}^{12} & \cdots & \frac{1-\alpha_k}{k-1}\mathbf{L}^{1k} \\ \frac{1-\alpha_1}{k-1}\mathbf{L}^{21} & 0 & \cdots & \frac{1-\alpha_k}{k-1}\mathbf{L}^{2k} \\ \vdots & \vdots & \ddots & \vdots \\ \frac{1-\alpha_1}{k-1}\mathbf{L}^{k1} & \frac{1-\alpha_2}{k-1}\mathbf{L}^{k2} & \cdots & 0 \end{bmatrix} \qquad (5.17)$$

and

$$\mathbf{G}^{n+1} = \mathbf{G}^n \mathbf{L} = \cdots = \mathbf{G}^i \mathbf{L}^{n-i+1} = \cdots = \mathbf{G}^0 \mathbf{L}^{n+1}, \qquad (5.18)$$

where $\mathbf{G}^0$ is a constant difference matrix and $\mathbf{L}$ is a constant matrix with a form given by

$$\mathbf{L} = \begin{bmatrix} 0 & \frac{1-\alpha_2}{k-1}\mathbf{L}^{12} & \cdots & \frac{1-\alpha_k}{k-1}\mathbf{L}^{1k} \\ \frac{1-\alpha_1}{k-1}\mathbf{L}^{21} & 0 & \cdots & \frac{1-\alpha_k}{k-1}\mathbf{L}^{2k} \\ \vdots & \vdots & \ddots & \vdots \\ \frac{1-\alpha_1}{k-1}\mathbf{L}^{k1} & \frac{1-\alpha_2}{k-1}\mathbf{L}^{k2} & \cdots & 0 \end{bmatrix}. \tag{5.19}$$

Because $\mathbf{L}^{ij}$ is obtained from $\mathbf{E}^{ij}$ and $\mathbf{L}^{ij} = \mathbf{D}_r^{ij-1}\mathbf{E}^{ij}$, each $l_{mn}^{ij} \in \mathbf{L}^{ij}$ satisfies

$$l_{mn}^{ij} \leq 1. \tag{5.20}$$

Furthermore, we obtain

$$\frac{1-\alpha_i}{k-1}l_{mn}^{ij} \in [0,1). \tag{5.21}$$

For each $\mathbf{L}^{ij}$, we have

$$\sum_n l_{mn}^{ij} = 1. \tag{5.22}$$

Here, $\|\bullet\|_\infty$ is adopted, and we obtain

$$\|\mathbf{L}\|_\infty = \max_t \{1-\alpha_t\}. \tag{5.23}$$

Because $\alpha_t \in (0,1]$, we have $\|\mathbf{L}\|_\infty < 1$, and $\rho(\mathbf{L}) \leq \|\mathbf{L}\|_\infty < 1$. By Lemma 2, we obtain

$$\lim_{n\to\infty} \mathbf{G}^{n+1} = \lim_{n\to\infty} \mathbf{G}^n\mathbf{L} = \cdots = \lim_{n\to\infty} \mathbf{G}^i\mathbf{L}^{n-i} = \cdots = \lim_{n\to\infty} \mathbf{G}^0\mathbf{L}^n = 0. \tag{5.24}$$

The convergence of Eq. (5.13) has accordingly been proven.

As shown above, the computational cost of the k-partite graph reinforcement process is $O(Tn^2)$, where n is the number of all vertices and T is the maximal iteration time.

5.4.2 Weight Learning for Multiple Views Using the *k*-Partite Graph

The *k*-partite graph is further used to determine the weights of multiple views. Given a query object Q and all other objects O_i from the 3-D object data set, we assume that all the representative views of each object have been generated (e.g., using unsupervised view selection methods). For the query object Q, the selected multiple views are $\mathbf{V}^Q = \{\mathbf{v}_1^q, \mathbf{v}_2^q, \ldots, \mathbf{v}_{n_q}^q\}$, and the corresponding initial weights for these views are $\Phi_Q^0 = \{\phi_1^q, \phi_2^q, \ldots, \phi_{n_q}^q\}$. Analogously, the selected multiple views are given by $\mathbf{V}^{O_i} = \{\mathbf{v}_1^{O_i}, \mathbf{v}_2^{O_i}, \ldots, \mathbf{v}_{n_{O_i}}^q\}$ and the initial weights $\Phi_{O_i}^0 = \{\phi_1^{O_i}, \phi_2^{O_i}, \ldots, \phi_{n_{O_i}}^{O_i}\}$ are generated for each O_i in the 3-D object data set.

The distance between the query Q and an object O_i is defined by

$$d(Q, O_i) = \sum_{t=1}^{n_q} \phi_t \times d\left(\mathbf{v}_t^q, \mathbf{V}^{O_i}\right), \tag{5.25}$$

where $(\mathbf{v}_t^q, \mathbf{V}^{O_i})$ is calculated according to

$$d\left(\mathbf{v}_t^q, \mathbf{V}^{O_i}\right) = \min_{\mathbf{v}^t \in \mathbf{V}^{O_i}} \left\{d\left(\mathbf{v}_t^q, \mathbf{v}^j\right)\right\}. \tag{5.26}$$

In each round of 3DOR, the top $k - 1$ returned samples are regarded as the pseudorelevant objects. The query object Q and these $k - 1$ objects are employed for constructing the *k*-partite graph G. In this *k*-partite graph, each partite denotes one 3-D object and each vertex in one partite denotes one representative view of the object. The edge between two vertices $\mathbf{v}_a^x$ and $\mathbf{v}_b^y$ is defined by

$$w_{ab}^{xy} = \exp\left(-\frac{d_{vv}^2\left(\mathbf{v}_a^x, \mathbf{v}_b^y\right)}{\sigma^2}\right), \tag{5.27}$$

where σ is a parameter set as the median value of the pairwise distances between all views in the database.

The *k*-partite graph reinforcement procedure is conducted in G using Eq. (5.13). After the convergence of the *k*-partite graph reinforcement, the weights for the representative views of the query object Q are updated by $\Phi_Q^* = \{\phi_1^{q*}, \phi_2^{q*}, \ldots, \phi_{n_q}^{q*}\}$. Algorithm 5.1 and Figure 5.6 illustrate

---

Algorithm 5.1 Weight optimization procedure for V3DOR with pseudo-relevant samples using the k-partite graph.

Step 1. Select representative views for the query object Q and other objects $\{O_1, O_2, \ldots, O_n\}$.

Step 2. Generate the initial weights for representative views.

Step 3. Conduct 3DOR.

Step 4. Construct the k-partite graph with Q and the top $k - 1$ pseudorelevant objects.

Step 5. Conduct the k-partite graph reinforcement with Eq. (5.13) and generate new weights for representative views of Q.

Step 6. Perform 3DOR again using the new weights.

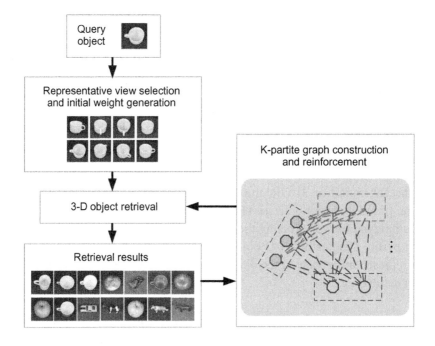

Figure 5.6 Schematic illustration of the weight optimization procedure using a k-partite graph for V3DOR.

the weight optimization procedure. These optimized weights can be more discriminative for the query object and used in the next round of 3DOR, as shown below.

$$d\left(\mathbf{O}_Q, \mathbf{O}_{O_i}\right) = \sum_{t=1}^{n_q} \phi_t^{q*} \times d\left(\mathbf{v}_t^q, \mathbf{V}^{O_i}\right). \tag{5.28}$$

5.5 SUMMARY

In this chapter, we focused on the representation of multiple views, including view feature extraction and multiple views weight learning. We first introduced analyses related to feature extraction methods, such as Zernike moments and Fourier descriptors. Next, we introduced the BoVF method and the BoRW method. Compared with traditional view features, the BoVF and BoRW descriptors exhibit better 3DOR performance. The last part of this chapter focused on the weight learning for multiple views, where we introduced our work on k-partite graph reinforcement learning. The pseudo-relevant feedback was employed to construct a k-partite graph and the reinforcement process was conducted to optimally determine the weights of multiple views.

We note that different objectives of 3DOR will lead to different requirements for view representation. For instance, there are many studies related to partial matching between 3-D objects that has a goal of partial 3DOR. The majority of existing view representation methods cannot leverage a single view feature or partial feature from different views of the entire 3-D object. We expect that future analyses of correlations among multiple views will attract more research attention. Upcoming work can be summarized as falling into one of the following two categories: feature extraction for global and local information descriptions and determining the correlations among multiple views.

REFERENCES

[1] Bustos B, Keim DA, Saupe D, Schreck T, Vranic DV. Feature-based similarity search in 3D object databases. ACM Comput Surv 2005;37(4):345-87.

[2] Paquet E, Rioux M, Murching A, Naveen T, Tabatabai A. Description of shape information for 2-D and 3-D objects. Signal Process Image Commun 2000;16(1):103-22.

[3] Ohbuchi R, Otagiri T, Ibato M, Takei T. Shape-similarity search of three-dimensional models using parameterized statistics. In: Proceedings of 10th Pacific Conference on Computer Graphics and Applications; 2002. p. 265-74.

[4] Saupe D, Vranic DV. 3D model retrieval with spherical harmonics and moments. In: Proceedings of the 23rd DAGM-Symposium on Pattern Recognition. Berlin: Springer; 2001. p. 392-7.

[5] Elad M, Tal A, Ar S. Content based retrieval of VRML objects—an iterative and interactive approach. In: ACM Conference on Multimedia. Vienna: Springer; 2001. p. 107-18.

[6] Osada R, Funkhouser T, Chazelle B, Dobkin D. Shape distributions. ACM Trans Graph 2002;21(4):807-32.

[7] Ip CY, Lapadat D, Sieger L, Regli WC. Using shape distributions to compare solid models. In: Proceedings of the 7th ACM Symposium on Solid Modeling and Applications; 2002. p. 273-80.

[8] Ohbuchi R, Minamitani T, Takei T. Shape-similarity search of 3D models by using enhanced shape functions. Int J Comput Appl Technol 2005;23(2):70-85.

[9] Vranic DV, Saupe D. Description of 3D-shape using a complex function on the sphere. Proc IEEE Int Conf Multimed Expo 2002;1:177-80.

[10] Healy DM, Rockmore DN, Kostelec PJ, Moore SSB. FFTs for the 2-sphere-improvements and variations. J Fourier Anal Appl 2003;9(4):341-85.

[11] Vranic D. An improvement of rotation invariant 3D shape descriptor based on functions on concentric spheres. Proc IEEE Int Conf Image Process 2003;3:757-60.

[12] Funkhouser T, Min P, Kazhdan M, Chen J, Halderman A, Dobkin D, et al. A search engine for 3D models. ACM Trans Graph 2003;22(1):83-105.

[13] Ankerst M, Kastenmuller G, Kregel HP, Seidl T. 3D shape histograms for similarity search and classification in spatial databases. In: Proceedings of the 6th International Symposium on Advances in Spatial Databases; 1999. p. 207-26.

[14] Paquet E, Rioux M. Nefertiti: a tool for 3-D shape databases management. Image Vis Comput 2000;108:387-93.

[15] Novotni M, Klein R. A geometric approach to 3D object comparison. In: Proceedings of the International Conference on Shape Modeling and Applications (SMI01); 2001. p. 167-75.

[16] Leifman G, Katz S, Meir R. Signatures of 3D models for retrieval. In: Proceedings of the 4th Israel-Korea Bi-National Conference on Geometric Modeling and Computer Graphics; 2003. p. 159-63.

[17] Kazhdan M, Chazelle B, Dobkin D, Funkhouser T, Rusinkiewicz S. A reflective symmetry descriptor for 3D models. Algorithmica 2003;38(1):201-25.

[18] Zaharia T, Preteux F. Three-dimensional shape-based retrieval within the MPEG-7 framework. In: Proceedings of the SPIE Conference on Nonlinear Image Processing and Pattern Analysis XII; 2001. p. 133-45.

[19] Shum HY, Hebert M, Ikeuchi K. On 3D shape similarity. In: Proceedings of the 1996 Conference on Computer Vision and Pattern Recognition; 1996. p. 526-31.

[20] Horn B. Extended Gaussian image. Proc IEEE 1984;72(12):1671-86.

[21] Khotanzad A, Hong YH. Invariant image recognition by Zernike moments. IEEE Trans Pattern Anal Mach Intell 1990;12(5):489-97.

[22] Bracewell R. The Fourier transform and its applications. 31999. New York: McGraw-Hill; 1986.

[23] Ohbuchi R, Furuya T. Accelerating bag-of-features sift algorithm for 3D model retrieval. In: Proceedings of SAMT Workshop on Semantic 3D Media; 2008.

[24] Furuya T, Ohbuchi R. Dense sampling and fast encoding for 3D model retrieval using bag-of-visual features. In: Proceedings of the ACM International Conference on Image and Video Retrieval; 2009.

[25] Ohbuchi R, Osada K, Furuya T, Banno T. Salient local visual features for shape based 3D model retrieval. In: Proceedings of IEEE Conference on Shape Modeling and Applications; 2008. p. 93-102.

[26] Ohbuchi R, Furuya T. Scale-weighted dense bag of visual features for 3D model retrieval from a partial view 3D model. In: Proceedings of IEEE ICCV Workshop on Search in 3D and Video; 2009.

[27] Gao Y, Wang M, Ji R, Zha Z, Shen J. K-partite graph reinforcement and its application in multimedia information retrieval. Inf Sci 2012;194:224-39.

[28] Hu MK. Visual pattern recognition by moment invariants. IRE Trans Inf Theory 1962;8:179-87.

[29] Abu-Mostafa YS, Psaltis D. Image normalization by complex moments. IEEE Trans Pattern Anal Mach Intell 1985;7(1):46-55.

[30] Ansary TF, Daoudi M, Vandeborre JP. A Bayesian 3D search engine using adaptive views clustering. IEEE Trans Multimed 2007;9(1):78-88.

[31] Gao Y, Wang M, Tao D, Ji R, Dai Q. 3D object retrieval and recognition with hypergraph analysis. IEEE Trans Image Process 2012;21(9):4290-303.

[32] Gao Y, Tang J, Hong R, Yan S, Dai Q, Zhang N, Chua T. Camera constraint-free view-based 3D object retrieval. IEEE Trans Image Process 2012;21(4):2269-81.

[33] Yap PT, Paramesran R, Ong SH. Image analysis by Krawtchouk moments. IEEE Trans Image Process 2003;12(11):1367-77.

[34] Chen DY, Tian XP, Shen YT, Ouhyoung M. On visual similarity based 3D model retrieval. Comput Graph Forum 2003;22(4):223-32.

[35] Daras P, Axenopoulos A. A 3D shape retrieval framework supporting multimodal queries. Int J Comput Vis 2010;89(2):229-47.

[36] Lazebnik S, Schmid C, Ponce J. Beyond bags of features: spatial pyramid matching for recognizing natural scene categories. Proc IEEE Comput Soc Conf Comput Vis Pattern Recogn 2006;2:2169-78.

[37] Nowak E, Jurie F, Triggs B. Sampling strategies for bag-of-features image classification. In: Proceedings of ECCV; 2006. p. 490-503.

[38] Yang J, Jiang Y, Hauptmann A, Ngo C. Evaluating bag-of-visual-words representations in scene classification. In: Proceedings of the International Workshop on Multimedia Information Retrieval; 2007. p. 197-206.

[39] Lowe D. Distinctive image features from scale-invariant keypoints. Int J Comput Vis 2004;60(2):91-110.

[40] Kullback S, Liebler R. On information and sufficiency. Ann Math Stat 1951;22:79-86.

[41] Gao Y, Yang Y, Dai Q, Zhang N. 3D object retrieval with bag-of-region-words. In: ACM Conference on Multimedia; 2010. p. 955-8.

[42] Steinbach M, Karypis G, Kumar V. A comparison of document clustering techniques. In: KDD Workshop TextMining; 2000.

[43] Rubner Y, Tomasi C, Guibas LJ. The earth mover's distance as a metric for image retrieval. Int J Comput Vis 2000;40(2):99-121.

[44] Saaty TL, Kainen PC. The four-color problem: assaults and conquest. New York: Dover; 1986. p. 12.

PART III

View-Based 3-D Object Comparison

View-based 3-D object comparison measures the distance and relevance among 3-D objects, which are the central task in V3DOR given the multiple views. We note that V3DOR differs significantly from traditional image retrieval, which is based on single image matching. This part of the book includes two chapters. Chapter 6 introduces the multiple-view distance metrics. In this chapter, the fundamental many-to-many matching distance measures are first provided, followed by the bipartite graph matching method and the statistical methods. Chapter 7 discusses recent progress in learning-based 3DOR methods, in which the learning methods are investigated in V3DOR for optimal distance metric learning, joint object relevance by leveraging a large data set of unlabeled data with the labeled samples, or both techniques.

CHAPTER 6

Multiple-View Distance Metric

6.1 INTRODUCTION

Distance metric is an important component of multimedia information retrieval task. In the case of V3DOR, the pairwise object distance measure is based on multiple views, which makes this measure distinct from traditional image retrieval tasks. Compared with the image retrieval task, which is based on the matching of two single images, multiple-view matching is more complex because of the high-order information contained in the multiple views of each 3-D object.

Multiple-view-based object matching can be regarded as a many-to-many matching problem, for which there are many existing methods, such as Hausdorff distance [1, 2] and the average distance between all view pairs. A straightforward technique is to directly employ these existing many-to-many matching methods. These methods have been employed in many studies, such as the matching methods in CMVD [3] and ED [4]. Although these methods are designed for many-to-many matching, the comparison between two groups of multiple views is different from existing many-to-many matching tasks because of the complex relationship among these multiple views.

Many recent studies of V3DOR have focused on the distance metric and several alternative methods [5–7] considering multiple views have been proposed. Generally, these methods can be divided into two categories: graph matching and statistical matching. In the graph matching method, the two groups of views to be compared can be formulated in a graph structure. Matching in this graph is conducted to calculate the distance/similarity between the two 3-D objects. In this part, we introduce our bipartite graph matching method [5], which formulates two groups of views in a bipartite graph. The second type of method is based on statistical matching. We use probabilistic analysis to make a comparison between two groups of views. Here, we further study the statistical matching methods used in studies by Ansary et al. [6] and Gao et al. [7]. Next, to determine the optimal distribution of the multiple views, we introduce a GMM-based method [8] to formulate a group of multiple views in a GMM. We next conduct GMM-based matching to measure the pairwise object distance.

This chapter is organized as follows. In Section 6.2, we introduce the fundamental distance measures of many-to-many matching for V3DOR, including the Hausdorff distance [1, 2], the minimal distance, the mean distance, and the sum-min distance. We next introduce the bipartite graph matching method [5] in Section 6.3. We further introduce the statistical matching methods [6–8] in Section 6.4. In the last part, we summarize this chapter.

6.2 FUNDAMENTAL MANY-TO-MANY DISTANCE MEASURES

Many-to-many matching methods have been investigated for decades. In this section, we introduce several popular fundamental many-to-many matching methods including Hausdorff distance [1, 2], the minimal distance, the mean distance, and the sum-min distance and their applications in V3DOR.

(1) Hausdorff distance [1, 2]

Hausdorff distance measures the distance between two subsets in a metric space. In Hausdorff distance, the distance between each point from one set and the closest point from the other set is determined. Then, Hausdorff distance is calculated as the maximal point-wise distance. If this minimal distance for each point is small, the overall Hausdorff distance will be small as well. Hausdorff distance is defined as

$$D(S_1, S_2) = \max \left\{ \begin{array}{l} \max_{e' \in S_1} \left\{ \min_{e'' \in S_2} d\left(e', e''\right) \right\} \\ \max_{e' \in S_2} \left\{ \min_{e'' \in S_1} d\left(e', e''\right) \right\} \end{array} \right\}. \qquad (6.1)$$

Here, S_1 and S_2 are the two subsets to be compared, and e' and e'' are the elements in these two subsets. $\min_{e'' \in S_2} d(e', e'')$ and $\min_{e'' \in S_1} d(e', e'')$ are the minimal distance for the element $e' \in S_1$ to S_2 and the minimal distance for the element $e' \in S_2$ to S_1, respectively.

To apply Hausdorff distance in V3DOR, the two groups of multiple views are regarded as two subsets S_1 and S_2, and each view is denoted by an element $e \in S$. With some view distance measures, the Hausdorff distance between two 3-D objects can be calculated.

Figure 6.1 illustrates the Hausdorff distance between two groups of views (samples).

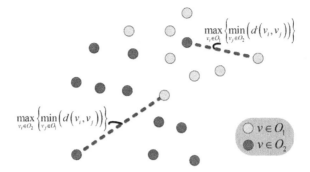

Figure 6.1 An example of the Hausdorff distance.

(2) **Minimal distance**

Given two groups of views V_1 and V_2 from two 3-D objects, the minimal distance is a measure of the minimal pairwise view distance. The minimal distance is defined as

$$D(V_1, V_2) = \min_{v' \in V_1, v'' \in V_2} d(v', v''), \qquad (6.2)$$

where v' and v'' are the views in V_1 and V_2, respectively. $d(v', v'')$ is the pairwise view distance between v' and v''. Figure 6.2 illustrates the minimal distance between two groups of views (samples).

(3) **Mean distance**

The mean distance is a measure of the average distance of all pairwise view distances between the two objects. The mean distance is defined as

$$D(V_1, V_2) = \frac{1}{|V_1||V_2|} \sum_{v' \in V_1} \sum_{v'' \in V_2} d(v', v''), \qquad (6.3)$$

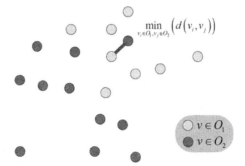

Figure 6.2 An example of the minimal distance.

where v' and v'' are the views in V_1 and V_2, respectively. $d(v', v'')$ is the pairwise view distance between v' and v''.

(4) Sum-min distance

The sum-min distance is a measure of the summation of the minimal distance for each view. The sum-min distance is defined as

$$D(V_1, V_2) = \frac{1}{|V_1|} \sum_{v' \in V_1} \min_{v'' \in V_2} d(v', v''). \qquad (6.4)$$

It is noted that the sum-min distance is asymmetric. In the above equation, $D(V_1, V_2)$ is the distance of V_2 to V_1.

An application of the sum-min distance is CMVD [3], in which the minimal distances for all views in the query object are employed to measure the distance between two 3-D objects.

6.3 BIPARTITE GRAPH MATCHING

Given two groups of multiple views for two 3-D objects, formulating a relationship between these objects is an important task for accurate matching. In this section, we introduce our bipartite graph matching method for 3DOR [5].

A bipartite graph $G = (U, V, E)$ [9] is a graph whose vertices are divided into two subsets U and V. Each edge e connects only two vertices from U and V. Figure 6.3 shows an example bipartite graph.

To address the matching task between two groups of multiple views, the relationship between two 3-D objects can be formulated in a bipartite graph structure. Figure 6.4 illustrates the framework in a study by Gao and collaborators [5]. As shown in the figure, the representative views are first selected from each 3-D object to construct the bipartite graph. Then, each selected view is associated with a corresponding weight. These weights can be updated using a random walk process. Then, two groups of selected views are formulated in one bipartite graph. In this bipartite graph, each vertex denotes one view, and the edge represents the similarity between two corresponding views. A proportional max-weighted bipartite matching process is conducted to measure the similarity between the two compared 3-D objects. The detailed algorithm is introduced below.

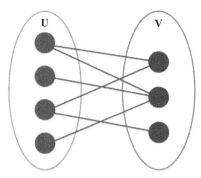

Figure 6.3 An example of the bipartite graph.

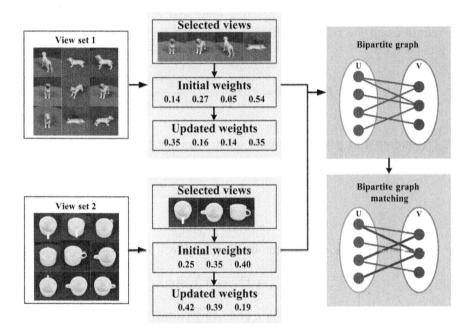

Figure 6.4 The framework of 3DOR by using the bipartite graph formulation [5].

6.3.1 View Selection and Weighting

Given two compared 3-D objects, O_1 and O_2, and the corresponding multiple views, $\{v_{11}, v_{12}, \ldots, v_{1n_1}\}$ and $\{v_{21}, v_{22}, \ldots, v_{2n_2}\}$, we first conduct view clustering to select the representative views. The HAC method [10] can be used here and the Zernike moment [11, 12] is employed as the view feature.

Let κ denote the number of generated view clusters. One representative view is selected from each view clustering, which is with the minimal distance to other views in the same cluster. Let $\{r_{11}, r_{12}, \ldots, r_{1\kappa}\}$ denote the κ selected views for O_1. Each selected view is assigned an initial weight $p^0_{rv_{1i}}$. The weight vector $P^0 = (p^0_{r_{11}}, p^0_{r_{12}}, \ldots, p^0_{r_{1\kappa}})$ is calculated according to

$$p^0_{r_{1i}} = \frac{|C(i)|}{|O_1|}, \tag{6.5}$$

where $|C(i)|$ is the number of views in the ith view cluster and $|O_1|$ is the number of views of the 3-D object O_1.

To generate a more accurate weight for each view, we construct a view graph to explore the relationship among these representative views. In this view graph, each vertex denotes one view and each edge connects two vertices using the relevance $R(r_{1i}, r_{1j})$ between the two views r_{1i} and r_{1j} calculated by

$$R(r_{1i}, r_{1j}) = \exp\left(-\frac{d(r_{1i}, r_{1j})^2}{\sigma^2}\right). \tag{6.6}$$

A random walk process is conducted in this view graph, and the transition probability from vertex r_{1i} to r_{1j} is calculated by

$$t(r_{1i}, r_{1j}) = \frac{R(r_{1i}, r_{1j})}{\sum_i r(r_{1i}, r_{1j})}. \tag{6.7}$$

The random walk process can be illustrated by

$$\begin{cases} p^{n+1}_{r_{11}} = \mu p^0_{r_{11}} + (1-\mu) \sum_{i \neq 1} t(r_{1i}, r_{11}) p^n_i \\ p^{n+1}_{r_{12}} = \mu p^0_{r_{12}} + (1-\mu) \sum_{i \neq 2} t(r_{1i}, r_{12}) p^n_i \\ \quad \vdots \\ p^{n+1}_{r_{1\kappa}} = \mu p^0_{r_{1\kappa}} + (1-\mu) \sum_{i \neq \kappa} t(r_{1i}, r_{1\kappa}) p^n_i \end{cases}, \tag{6.8}$$

where μ is a parameter, and this procedure converges after a few iterations. Here, we denote the new weights by $\{p^f_{r_{11}}, p^f_{r_{12}}, \ldots, p^f_{r_{1\kappa}}\}$.

With these updated weights for all selected views, we can construct the bipartite graph, as detailed below.

6.3.2 Bipartite Graph Construction

Given two groups of multiple views $X = \{r_{11}, r_{12}, \ldots, r_{1n_1}\}$ and $Y = \{r_{21}, r_{22}, \ldots, r_{2n_2}\}$, and the corresponding weights $\{p_{r_{11}}^f, p_{r_{12}}^f, \ldots, p_{r_{1n_1}}^f\}$ and $\{p_{r_{21}}^f, p_{r_{22}}^f, \ldots, p_{r_{2n_2}}^f\}$, where n_1 and n_2 are the numbers of selected views for O_1 and O_2, respectively, we can construct an object bipartite graph. Here, we assume $n_1 \geq n_2$ and we add $n_1 - n_2$ empty elements in Y. We accordingly obtain a set Y' with n_1 elements. We construct a bipartite graph $G = \{X, Y', \mathbf{E}\}$ in which each vertex denotes one element from X or Y and each edge $w_{i,j}$ $(i, j = 1, 2, \ldots, n_1)$ connects two vertices. Let $d(r_{1i}, r_{2j})$ denote the distance between r_{1i} and r_{2j}, and let $p_{r_{1i}}^f$ and $p_{r_{2j}}^f$ denote the corresponding weights. $w_{i,j}$ is calculated according to

$$
w_{ij} = \begin{cases} \frac{1}{2}(p_{r_{1i}}^f + p_{r_{2j}}^f) \times d(r_{1i}, r_{2j}) & \text{if } j \leq n_2 \\ 0 & \text{otherwise.} \end{cases} \tag{6.9}
$$

6.3.3 Bipartite Graph Matching

Max-weighted bipartite graph matching aims to determine the maximum cardinality for a weighted bipartite graph. In a graph $G = (U, V, \mathbf{E})$, let $\Lambda_k \in \Lambda$ be a bipartite graph matching, and let $a_k(i)$ and $b_k(i)$ be two matching nodes in λ_k in which $a_k(i) \in U$, $b_k(i) \in V$, and $1 \leq i \leq n$. In a max-weighted bipartite matching $\Lambda_{\mathbf{m}}$, each vertex in one subset is matched to only one vertex in the other subset. We employ the Kuhn-Munkres method [9] to determine the max-weighted bipartite matching in G. Here, we modify the correlation between two vertices as $c_{ij} = \epsilon - w_{ij}$ and $\epsilon \geq \max(w_{ij})$. The missing edges should be given a high cost, that is, ϵ. The objective function of the max-weighted bipartite matching can be written as

$$
\Lambda_{\mathbf{m}} = \arg \max_{\Lambda_k \in \Lambda} \sum_{1 \leq i \leq n} c_{a_k(i), b_k(i)} = \arg \max_{\Lambda_k \in \Lambda} \sum_{1 \leq i \leq n} (\epsilon - w_{a_k(i), b_k(i)}). \tag{6.10}
$$

The output max-weighted bipartite matching result is regarded as the similarity between the two 3-D objects, which can be employed for 3DOR. The merit of the bipartite graph formation lies in its capacity to measure the overall similarity between two separated sets of views.

6.4 STATISTICAL MATCHING

Distinct from the graph matching method, statistical matching methods aim to calculate the similarity/probability through statistical methods. In the first two parts of this section, we introduce the adaptive view clustering (AVC) method [6] and the camera constraint-free method (CCFV) [7], which measures the probability between two objects. Next, we introduce a Markov chain method [13]. In the fourth part, we introduce a GMM method [8], in which the distribution of multiple views is formulated in a GMM, and the GMM comparison measures the distance between the two 3-D objects.

6.4.1 Adaptive View Clustering

A Bayesian approach (AVC) is introduced in a study by Ansary et al. in [6], in which the distance between two 3-D objects is formulated in a probabilistic way. In AVC, characteristic views are first selected and then the object matching is conducted using these selected views. Given a query Q and another object O, the objective of 3DOR is to determine the objects that are highly probable—where the probability is given by $p(O_i|Q)$—of being close to Q. Given the selected views, $p(O_i|Q)$ can be rewritten as

$$p(O_i|Q) = \sum_{k=1}^{K} p(O_i|V_Q^k)p(V_Q^k|Q),\qquad(6.11)$$

where K is the number of views in Q.

6.4.2 CCFV

The CCFV method [7] is distinct from AVC in that it considers not only the positive matching between views but also the negative matching. For a query object Q with the views $V^Q = \{v_1^Q, v_2^Q, \ldots, v_m^Q\}$ and an object O with the views $V^O = \{v_1^O, v_2^O, \ldots, v_n^O\}$, the relationship between Q and O can be defined by a binary variable Δ as follows:

$$\begin{cases} \Delta = 1 & O \text{ is relevant to } Q \\ \Delta = 0 & O \text{ is irrelevant to } Q. \end{cases}\qquad(6.12)$$

The objective of 3DOR is to find the objects with $\Delta = 1$. It is noted that an object O can be either relevant or irrelevant to Q. Therefore, we can measure the similarity between Q and O by considering the two likelihood ratios as follows:

$$S(Q, O) = p(O|Q, \Delta = 1) - p(O|Q, \Delta = 0).\qquad(6.13)$$

In the above function, $p(O|Q, \Delta = 1)$ indicates the probability of O given Q when they are relevant and $p(O|Q, \Delta = 0)$ is when Q and O are irrelevant.

Therefore, the objective function can be rewritten as follows:

$$r = \arg \max_{O \in DB} S(Q, O)$$
$$= \arg \max_{O \in DB} p(O|Q, \Delta = 1) - p(O|Q, \Delta = 0). \qquad (6.14)$$

Then, a large r value indicates a high relevance between Q and O, which can be used to rank all the objects in descending order to recover the 3DOR results.

To measure the two likelihood ratios, the CCFV method is composed of three steps, as shown in   Figure 6.5. All the views for the query object Q are first grouped into clusters, and the query Gaussian model is generated from each view cluster. A positive matching model and a negative matching model are trained with positive and negative matched view pairs, respectively. Then the similarity between Q and O is generated using Eq. (6.13).

6.4.2.1 View Clustering and Query Model Training

Given m views $V^Q = \{v_1^Q, v_2^Q, \ldots, v_m^Q\}$ of Q, the Zernike moments [6, 11, 14] are first extracted for each view. Then the HAC method [10] is conducted

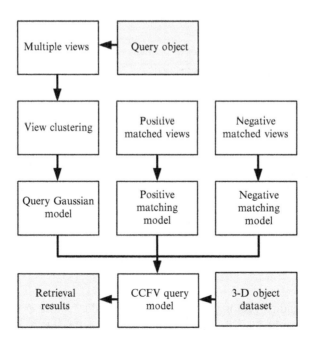

Figure 6.5 The framework of the CCFV method [7].

to group these views into view clusters, and one representative view is selected from each cluster. The representative view set of O is denoted by $V^{\bar{O}} = \{v_1^{\bar{O}}, v_2^{\bar{O}}, \ldots, v_\tau^{\bar{O}}\}$. A Gaussian model for the feature distribution can be obtained for each view cluster.

Let $\mathbf{x}$ denote the feature of training views, the GMM $p(\mathbf{x}|\Theta) = \sum_{i=1}^{n_g} \omega_i g_i(\mathbf{x}|\mu_i, \sigma_i^2)$ is generated, where $g_i(\mathbf{x}|\mu_i, \sigma_i^2)$ is the ith Gaussian component, ω_i is the weight of the ith Gaussian component, and n_g is the number of Gaussian models.

The probability of one view in the ith Gaussian component is calculated according to

$$g_i(\mathbf{x}|\mu_i, \sigma_i^2) = \frac{1}{\sqrt{2\pi}\sigma_i} \exp\left(-\frac{(d(\mathbf{x}, \mu_i))^2}{2\sigma_i^2}\right), \tag{6.15}$$

where $d(\mathbf{x}, \mu_i)$ is the Euclidian distance between $\mathbf{x}$ and μ_i and μ_i and σ_i are the parameters of the Gaussian model.

It is noted that the number of views is too small compared with the dimension of the feature. To overcome this problem, each Gaussian component $p(\mathbf{x}) = g_i(\mathbf{x}|\mu_i, \sigma_i^2)$ is calculated as follows

$$\omega_i = \frac{n_i}{m}, \tag{6.16}$$

$$\mu_i = \frac{1}{n_i} \sum_{k=1}^{n_i} \psi_k^Q, \tag{6.17}$$

$$\sigma_i^2 = \frac{1}{n_i - 1} \sum_{k=1}^{n_i} \left(d(\psi_k^Q - \mu_i)\right)^2, \tag{6.18}$$

where m is the number of views in Q, n_i is the number of views in the ith cluster, and $\psi_{k\,(k=1,2,\ldots,n_i)}^Q$ are the feature vectors of views in the ith cluster.

6.4.2.2 Positive and Negative Matching Models

There are two possible results for the matching between two views—relevant or irrelevant—which are denoted by $\Delta = 1$ and $\Delta = 0$, respectively.

Given a feature vector ψ from one object and a feature ϕ from the other object, the conditional density functions with different Δ values can be calculated according to

$$p(\phi|\psi, \Delta = 1) = \mathcal{N}(\phi|\psi, \sigma_{\text{pos}}^2) \tag{6.19}$$

and

$$p(\phi|\psi, \Delta = 0) = \mathcal{N}(\phi|\psi, \sigma_{\text{neg}}^2), \tag{6.20}$$

where σ_{pos}^2 and σ_{neg}^2 are the variances for the two matching models.

σ_{pos}^2 and σ_{neg}^2 are calculated according to

$$\sigma_{\text{pos}}^2 = \frac{1}{n_{\text{pos}} - 1} \sum_{k=1}^{n_{\text{pos}}} \left(d\left(\mathbf{v}_{\text{pos}}(k, 1), \mathbf{v}_{\text{pos}}(k, 2)\right)\right)^2 \tag{6.21}$$

and

$$\sigma_{\text{neg}}^2 = \frac{1}{n_{\text{neg}} - 1} \sum_{k=1}^{n_{\text{neg}}} \left(d\left(\mathbf{v}_{\text{neg}}(k, 1), \mathbf{v}_{\text{neg}}(k, 2)\right)\right)^2, \tag{6.22}$$

where n_{pos} and n_{neg} are the numbers of positive and negative matched view pairs, $\mathbf{v}_{\text{pos}}(k, 1)$ and $\mathbf{v}_{\text{pos}}(k, 2)$ are the kth positive matched view pair, and $\mathbf{v}_{\text{neg}}(k, 1)$ and $\mathbf{v}_{\text{neg}}(k, 2)$ are the kth negative matched view pair. One thousand pairs of positive matched views and 2000 pairs of negative matched views are selected to train the positive and negative matching models in Gao et al. [7]. The average pairwise view distances in the two training sets ($D_{\text{POS}}, D_{\text{NEG}}$) can be calculated according to

$$D_{\text{POS}} = \frac{1}{n_{\text{pos}}} \sum_{k=1}^{n_{\text{pos}}} \left(d\left(\mathbf{v}_{\text{pos}}(k, 1), \mathbf{v}_{\text{pos}}(k, 2)\right)\right) \tag{6.23}$$

and

$$D_{\text{NEG}} = \frac{1}{n_{\text{neg}}} \sum_{k=1}^{n_{\text{neg}}} \left(d\left(\mathbf{v}_{\text{neg}}(k, 1), \mathbf{v}_{\text{neg}}(k, 2)\right)\right). \tag{6.24}$$

6.4.2.3 Calculation of the Similarity Between Q and O $S(Q, O)$

To calculate $S(Q, O)$, both $p(O|Q, \Delta = 1)$ and $p(O|Q, \Delta = 0)$ are required, which are introduced here.

Given an object O and the query Q, $p(O|Q, \Delta = 1)$ is calculated according to

$$
\begin{aligned}
p\,(O|Q, \Delta = 1) &= p(V^O | V^Q, \Delta = 1) \\
&= p\left(\{v_1^O, v_2^O, \ldots, v_n^O\} | V^Q, \Delta = 1 \right) \\
&= p\left(\{\phi_1^{\bar{O}}, \phi_2^{\bar{O}}, \ldots, \phi_\tau^{\bar{O}}\} | \{\psi_1^Q, \psi_2^Q, \ldots, \psi_m^Q\}, \Delta = 1 \right),
\end{aligned}
$$
(6.25)

which can be rewritten according to

$$
p(O|Q, \Delta = 1) = \sum_{k=1}^{n_g} \left\{ p(\phi_1^{\bar{O}}, \phi_2^{\bar{O}}, \ldots, \phi_\tau^{\bar{O}} | \psi_k^Q, \Delta = 1) p(\psi_k^Q | Q) \right\}.
$$
(6.26)

Here, $p(\phi_1, \phi_2, \ldots, \phi_n | \psi_k, \Delta = 1)$ can be calculated according to

$$
p(\phi_1^{\bar{O}}, \phi_2^{\bar{O}}, \ldots, \phi_\tau^{\bar{O}} | \psi_k^Q, \Delta = 1) = \sum_{i=1}^{\tau} p(\phi_i^{\bar{O}} | \psi_k^Q, \Delta = 1).
$$
(6.27)

Generally, when the two objects O and Q are relevant, each Gaussian component of Q can match views in O. Therefore, the maximal probability can be employed in Eq. (6.27):

$$
p(\phi_1^{\bar{O}}, \phi_2^{\bar{O}}, \ldots, \phi_\tau^{\bar{O}} | \psi_k^Q, \Delta = 1) = \max_{i=1,2,\ldots,\tau} p(\phi_i^{\bar{O}} | \psi_k^Q, \Delta = 1),
$$
(6.28)

where

$$
p(\phi_i^{\bar{O}} | \psi_k^Q, \Delta = 1) = \mathcal{N}(\phi_i^{\bar{O}} | \mu_k, \sigma_{\text{pos}}^2).
$$
(6.29)

Another observation is that when the two compared views are similar enough, they are positively matched. If the two compared views are dissimilar enough from each other, they cannot be positively matched. Then, we can write Eq. (6.29) as

$$
p(\phi^{\bar{O}} | \psi_k^Q, \Delta = 1) = \frac{1}{\sqrt{2\pi}\sigma_{\text{pos}}} \exp\left(-\frac{d_{\text{pos}}(\phi^{\bar{O}}, \mu_k)^2}{2\sigma_{\text{pos}}^2} \right),
$$
(6.30)

where $d_{\text{pos}}(\phi, \mu_k)$ is computed according to

$$
d_{\text{pos}}(\phi^{\bar{O}}, \mu_k) = \begin{cases} 0 & \text{if } d(\phi^{\bar{O}}, \mu_k) < D_{\text{POS}} \\ \infty & \text{if } d(\phi^{\bar{O}}, \mu_k) > D_{\text{NEG}} \\ d(\phi^{\bar{O}}, \mu_k) & \text{otherwise.} \end{cases}
$$
(6.31)

$p(O|Q, \Delta = 0)$ can be calculated in a similar way. When two views are too dissimilar from each other, these two views are regarded as being negatively matched. Letting σ_{neg} denote the variance of a negatively matched sample distribution, $p(O|Q, \Delta = 0)$ can be obtained according to

$$p(O|Q, \Delta = 0) = p(V^O|V^Q, \Delta = 0)$$

$$= p\left(\{v_1^O, v_2^O, \ldots, v_n^O\}|V^Q, \Delta = 0\right)$$

$$= p\left(\{\phi_1^{\bar{O}}, \phi_2^{\bar{O}}, \ldots, \phi_\tau^{\bar{O}}\}|\{\psi_1^Q, \psi_2^Q, \ldots, \psi_m^Q\}, \Delta = 0\right)$$

$$= \sum_{k=1}^{n_{gm}} \left\{ p(\phi_1^{\bar{O}}, \phi_2^{\bar{O}}, \ldots, \phi_\tau^{\bar{O}}|\psi_k^Q, \Delta = 0)p(\psi_k^Q|Q) \right\}, \quad (6.32)$$

where

$$p(\phi_1^{\bar{O}}, \phi_2^{\bar{O}}, \ldots, \phi_\tau^{\bar{O}}|\psi_k^Q, \Delta = 0) = \max_{i=1,2,\ldots,\tau} p(\phi_i^{\bar{O}}|\psi_k^Q, \Delta = 0). \quad (6.33)$$

Here, $p(\phi_i^{\bar{O}}|\psi_k^Q, \Delta = 0)$ is calculated according to

$$p(\phi_i^{\bar{O}}|\psi_k^Q, \Delta = 0) = \frac{1}{\sqrt{2\pi}\sigma_{neg}} \exp\left(-\frac{d_{neg}(\phi^{\bar{O}}, \mu_k)^2}{2\sigma_{neg}^2}\right), \quad (6.34)$$

where $d_{neg}(\phi^{\bar{O}}, \mu_k)$ is computed according to

$$d_{neg}(\phi^{\bar{O}}, \mu_k) = \begin{cases} \infty & \text{if } d(\phi^{\bar{O}}, \mu_k) < D_{POS} \\ 0 & \text{if } d(\phi^{\bar{O}}, \mu_k) > D_{NEG} \\ D_{NEG} - d(\phi^{\bar{O}}, \mu_k) & \text{otherwise.} \end{cases} \quad (6.35)$$

With obtained values of $p(O|Q, \Delta = 1) - p(O|Q, \Delta = 0)$ for all objects O, the retrieval results can be placed in a descending order.

6.4.2.4 Analysis of Computational Cost

Here, we discuss the computational cost of CCFV. The view clustering procedure costs $O(n^2 \log m)$, where m is the number of views in Q. In the CCFV framework, the computational cost scales as $O(\bar{K}^2 N)$, where $\bar{K}$ is the average number of clusters for each 3-D object, and N is the number of all objects in the dataset.

6.4.3 Markov Chain

Considering the relationship among multiple views for each 3-D object, we propose a Markov chain-based statistical pairwise object distance measure for 3DOR in [13]. In this method, the Markov chain is used to explore the statistical characteristics of the multiple images for one 3-D object.

Here, we first introduce the quasi-histogram method [15]. Letting $H = [H_1, H_2, \ldots, H_m]^T$ denote the m-bin histogram of a view, the corresponding quasi-histogram can be calculated according to

$$H_k^q = \min \left\{ m : \widetilde{H}_m \leq \frac{k}{K_H} \right\} \quad (1 \leq k \leq K_H), \quad (6.36)$$

where $\widetilde{H}$ is the cumulative histogram corresponding to H, and K_H is the length of the quasi-histogram. In this definition, the quasi-histogram H^q can be regarded as a state sequence reflecting the view information. For the feature for a given view, each bin of the original histogram can be treated as a random variable with an exponential distribution and the quasi-histogram can be characterized by a Markov chain, as introduced in a study by Li and collaborators [15].

Given n_o objects with m images for each object, the sets of histograms and the quasi-histograms for the m views of the kth object O_k can be written as $H_k = \{H_{k1}, H_{k2}, \ldots, H_{km}\}$ and $H_k^q = \{H_{k1}^q, H_{k2}^q, \ldots, H_{km}^q\}$. Here, based on the assumption that the quasi-histograms of the m images for one 3-D object can be stochastically generated by using the same Markov chain, n_o Markov chains, that is, $\upsilon_1, \upsilon_2, \ldots, \upsilon_{n_o}$, can be trained [15], in which each Markov chain υ_i describes the ith 3-D object using the quasi-histogram H_k^q.

Given these Markov chain-based features, the distance between two 3-D objects can be measured using the Kullback-Leibler (KL) divergence [16]. The KL divergence between two Markov chains υ_i and υ_j can be calculated according to

$$d_{\mathrm{KL}}\left(\upsilon_i, \upsilon_j\right) = \sum_{X \in \mathrm{A}} P\left(X|\upsilon_i\right) \log \frac{P\left(X|\upsilon_i\right)}{P\left(X|\upsilon_j\right)}, \quad (6.37)$$

where X is the observation sequence and A is the set of observation symbols.

The Monte Carlo method is employed here to numerically approximate the KL divergence between two distributions. Given m observation sequences $X_1, X_2, \ldots, X_m$ for υ_i, the KL divergence can be rewritten as

$$d_{\mathrm{KL}}\left(v_i, v_j\right) = \frac{1}{m} \sum_{s=1}^{m} \log \frac{P\left(X_s | v_i\right)}{P\left(X_s | v_j\right)}$$

$$= \frac{1}{m} \sum_{s=1}^{m} \left\{ \log \left[P\left(X_s | v_i\right) \right] - \log \left[P\left(X_s | v_j\right) \right] \right\}. \quad (6.38)$$

Given the quasi-histogram features for multiple views, that is, $H_i^q, i = 1, \ldots, n_o$, the divergence between two 3-D objects can be measured according to

$$d_{\mathrm{KL}}\left(v_i, v_j\right) = \frac{1}{m} \sum_{s=1}^{m} \left\{ \log \left[P\left(H_{is}^q | v_i\right) \right] - \log \left[P\left(H_{is}^q | v_j\right) \right] \right\}. \quad (6.39)$$

Then, the symmetric KL divergence can be calculated as the distance between the two 3-D objects being compared by

$$d_{\mathrm{MC}}\left(O_i, O_j\right) = d_{\mathrm{KL}}\left(v_i, v_j\right) + d_{\mathrm{KL}}\left(v_j, v_i\right). \quad (6.40)$$

6.4.4 Gaussian Mixture Model Formulation

To better formulate the feature distribution of multiple views, a discriminatory probabilistic modeling method based on GMM is introduced in [8]. This technique, which is in place of direct view matching, can formulate multiple view-based 3-D objects. In this method, the comparison between two 3-D objects is conducted using the KL divergence [16] between two GMMs. Figure 6.6 illustrates the framework of the discriminatory probabilistic modeling of 3-D objects with GMM, including four main steps: global GMM generation, generative adaptation of GMM, discriminatory adaptation of GMM, and determining the weights for multiple GMMs. In this part, the conventional GMM training is first introduced, followed by a discussion of the four procedures for the GMM-based discriminatory probabilistic modeling method.

6.4.4.1 Conventional GMM Training

GMM [17] has been widely used in computer vision and multimedia applications, such as speech analysis [18], background subtraction [19], and tracking [20]. For conventional GMM training, given n views $\{v_1, v_2, \ldots, v_{n_v}\}$ with a d-dimensional feature, the GMM with K components can be generated according to

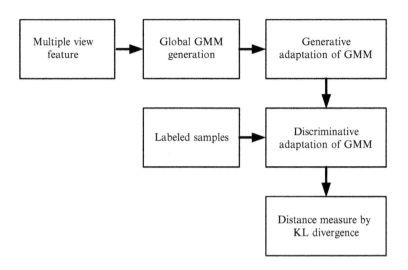

Figure 6.6 The framework of the discriminative probabilistic modeling using the GMM method [8].

$$
\begin{aligned}
p(x|\Theta) &= \sum_{k=1}^{K} \pi_k g(x; \mu_k, \Sigma_k) \\
&= \sum_{k=1}^{K} \frac{\pi_k}{\sqrt{(2\pi)^d |\Sigma_k|}} \exp\{-\frac{1}{2}(x - \mu_k)^T \Sigma_k^{-1}(x - \mu_k)\}
\end{aligned}
$$

(6.41)

where $\Theta = \{\pi_1, \pi_2, \ldots, \pi_K, \mu_1, \mu_2, \ldots, \mu_K, \Sigma_1, \Sigma_2, \ldots, \Sigma_K\}$ denotes the GMM parameters, which can be calculated using the expectation maximization (EM) algorithm [21] via the following two steps:

Expectation step:

$$
w_{jk} = \frac{\pi_k g(x_j; \mu_k, \Sigma_k)}{\sum_{k=1}^{K} \pi_k g(x_j; \mu_k, \Sigma_k)}.
$$

(6.42)

Maximization step:

$$
\pi_k = \frac{1}{n_v} \sum_{j=1}^{n_v} w_{jk},
$$

(6.43)

$$
\mu_k = \frac{\sum_{j=1}^{n_v} w_{jk} x_j}{\sum_{j=1}^{n_v} w_{jk}}
$$

(6.44)

and

$$\Sigma_k = \frac{\sum_{j=1}^{n_v} w_{jk}(x - \mu_k)(x - \mu_k)^T}{\sum_{j=1}^{n_v} w_{jk}}. \qquad (6.45)$$

These two steps are iterated until the process converges. Additional details related to GMM can be found in Bishop [22].

6.4.4.2 Generative Adaptation of GMM

A well-trained GMM generally requires adequate training samples. It is noted that the number of multiple views for each 3-D object is too small compared with the dimension of the feature. Therefore, directly generating a GMM may suffer from the overfitting problem. For example, a popularly used feature, the Zernike moments has 49 dimensions. For this feature, tens or hundreds of samples are not adequate to generate a satisfactory GMM. In these circumstances, a common solution is to train a global GMM first and then adapt the global model for each object individually. This technique is called the universal background model (UBM) [23–25].

To conduct the generative adaptation of GMM, the GMM is trained for each object by adapting the means of the global GMM and retaining the mixture weights and covariance matrices. Here, the means of the global GMM are denoted by $\bar{\mu}_1, \bar{\mu}_2, \ldots, \bar{\mu}_K$, and they are adapted using the maximum *a posteriori* (MAP) adaptation with conjugate priors [23]. Thus, the adaptive means for each 3-D object can be determined by maximizing the following objective function:

$$\log p(\mu_1, \mu_2, \ldots, \mu_K, V) = \sum_{k=1}^{K} \log g\left(\mu_k; \bar{\mu}_k, \frac{\Sigma_k}{r}\right)$$
$$+ \sum_{i=1}^{n_v} \log \sum_{k=1}^{K} g(v_k; \mu_k, \Sigma_k), \quad (6.46)$$

where $V = \{v_1, v_2, \ldots, v_{n_v}\}$ are the views of one 3-D object. In this procedure, the conjugate prior for the kth mean μ_k is itself and $g(\mu_k; \bar{\mu}_k, \frac{\Sigma_k}{r})$ with a covariance matrix shrunk by a smoothing parameter r. The joint distribution function can be optimized in the same way as the EM approach.

The expectation step is

$$\Pr(k|v_i) = \frac{\pi_k g(v_i; \mu_k, \Sigma_k)}{\sum_{k=1}^{K} \pi_k g(v_i; \mu_k, \Sigma_k)} \qquad (6.47)$$

and

$$n_k = \sum_{i=1}^{n_v} \Pr(k|v_i). \qquad (6.48)$$

The maximization step is

$$E(\mu_k) = \frac{1}{n_v} \sum_{i=1}^{n_v} \Pr(k|v_i)v_i \qquad (6.49)$$

and

$$\mu_k = \alpha_k E(\mu_k) + (1 - \alpha_k)\bar{\mu}_k, \qquad (6.50)$$

where $\alpha_k = \frac{n_k}{n_k + r}$.

The adaptation procedure can interpolate between the means μ_k and the maximum likelihood parameters $E(\mu_k)$. If the probabilistic count n_k is large for one Gaussian component, the weight α_k will tend toward 1 and the adapted parameters will emphasize the new statistics of the given data; otherwise, the adapted parameters will be determined by the UBM. This adaptation process iterates until it converges. It is noted that in the generative adaptation step, only the means of the GMMs are adapted for each 3-D object.

6.4.4.3 Discriminative Adaptation of GMM

In the last procedure, it is noted that the model obtained is the general model for each 3-D object from the UBM directly. Furthermore, the covariance matrices were identical. To be more discriminative for each individual 3-D object, an additional discriminative adaptation is required. Here, we let $\Theta_i = \{\pi_1, \ldots, \pi_K, \mu_{i,1}, \ldots, \mu_{i,K}, \Sigma_1, \ldots, \Sigma_K\}$ denote the GMM of the ith object from the last step and an adaptation of the mean vectors of the GMMs is imposed to further enhance the discriminative ability of each 3-D object. A linear transformation matrix is introduced to update the GMM: Θ_i becomes $\Theta_i' = \{\pi_1, \pi_2, \ldots, \pi_K, \mathbf{A}\mu_{i,1}, \mathbf{A}\mu_{i,2}, \ldots, \mathbf{A}\mu_{i,K}, \Sigma_1, \Sigma_2, \ldots, \Sigma_K\}$. Here, $\mathbf{A}$ conducts a linear transformation on the mean vectors.

To measure the distance between two different 3-D objects, the KL divergence [16] is employed here, which is the most widely adopted distance measure. The KL divergence is defined as

$$D(p(x|\Theta_i')\|p(x|\Theta_j')) = \int p(x|\Theta_i') \log \frac{p(x|\Theta_i')}{p(x|\Theta_j')} dx. \qquad (6.51)$$

It is noted that it is difficult to calculate the KL divergence between two GMMs directly as this process is not analytically tractable. One common solution is to employ the upper bound of the KL divergence. Under the log-sum inequality, we have

$$D(p(x|\Theta_i')\|p(x|\Theta_j')) \le \sum_{k=1}^{K} \pi_k D(g(x; A\mu_{i,k}, \Sigma_k)\|g(x; A\mu_{j,k}, \Sigma_k)). \qquad (6.52)$$

Now, the KL divergence between the two Gaussian components $g(x; A\mu_{i,k}, \Sigma_k)$ and $g(x; A\mu_{j,k}, \Sigma_k)$ can be derived as

$$D(g(x; A\mu_{i,k}, \Sigma_k)\|g(x; A\mu_{j,k}, \Sigma_k)) = (\mu_{i,k} - \mu_{j,k})^T A^T \Sigma_k^{-1} A(\mu_{i,k} - \mu_{j,k}). \qquad (6.53)$$

$\sum_{k=1}^{K} \pi_k D(g(x; A\mu_{i,k}, \Sigma_k)\|g(x; A\mu_{j,k}, \Sigma_k))$ can be replaced by Div_{ij} for notational simplicity. The task here is changed to optimize A using the label information.

Here, the kNN classifier error rate is taken into consideration using the method introduced in Goldberger et al. [26] to optimize the leave-one-out performance of the labeled data. A differentiable cost function is defined based on stochastic neighbor assignments in the transformed space. Each object x_i can select another object x_j as its neighbor with some probability p_{ij}, and inherits its class label from the point it selects. p_{ij} is defined as

$$p_{ij} = \frac{\exp(-\text{Div}_{ij})}{\sum_{k \ne i} \exp(-\text{Div}_{kj})} \qquad (6.54)$$

and the objective is to maximize the expected number of objects that can be correctly classified:

$$f(A) = \sum_i \sum_{j \in C_i} p_{ij} = \sum_i \sum_{j \in C_i} \frac{\exp(-\text{Div}_{ij})}{\sum_{k \ne i} \exp(-\text{Div}_{kj})}, \qquad (6.55)$$

where $\mathcal{C}_i$ denotes the set of objects in the same class as the ith sample. Differentiating f with respect to $\mathbf{A}$ can lead to

$$\frac{\partial f}{\partial \mathbf{A}} = \sum_i \sum_{j \in \mathcal{C}_i} p_{ij} \left(q_{ij} - \sum_k p_{ik} q_{ik} \right), \tag{6.56}$$

where

$$q_{ij} = \sum_{k=1}^K \pi_k \Sigma_k^{-1} \mathbf{A} (\mu_{ik} - \mu_{jk})(\mu_{ik} - \mu_{jk})^T. \tag{6.57}$$

The above optimization problem can be solved with a gradient descent process:

$$\mathbf{A}_{t+1} = \mathbf{A}_t - \eta \frac{\partial f}{\partial \mathbf{A}} |_{\mathbf{A}=\mathbf{A}_t}. \tag{6.58}$$

6.4.4.4 Learning the Weights for Multiple GMMs

In GMM, it is difficult to select the number of Gaussian components. A small number of Gaussian components may lead to a model that is not discriminatory, while a large number of Gaussian components may produce a model that loses relevance among different samples. Most existing studies empirically set a fixed number of Gaussian components for the GMM or set a number using information-theoretic methods, that is, a minimum description length [27]. It is noted that these methods cannot be directly used in 3DOR because GMMs with different numbers of components represent different granularities of data distributions. To overcome this problem, a multiple GMM approach is introduced in [8] to illustrate the data distribution in different granularities. First, multiple GMMs with different numbers of Gaussian components are generated and the optimal weights for multiple GMM combinations are determined using the labeled data, which can be obtained from the user relevance feedback.

Here, let Ω denote the pool of Gaussian component numbers. Given all these trained GMMs, the distance between two objects can be calculated by linearly combining the multiple distances from different corresponding GMM pairs:

$$D_{ij} = \sum_{k \in \Omega} \lambda_k D_{ij}^{(k)}. \tag{6.59}$$

Here, λ_k is the weight for the kth GMM.

The distances from different GMM granularities should have different weights because of their ability to discriminate. Therefore, the weights used for combining different GMMs should be optimally selected. To determine the optimal weights, the aim is to minimize the distances of objects belonging to the same classes and maximize the distances of the objects belonging to different classes:

$$\min_{\lambda} \sum_{(O_i,O_j)\in Sa} D_{ij} - \sum_{(O_i,O_j)\in Dif} D_{ij}$$

$$\text{s.t.} \quad \lambda_k \geq 0, \sum_{k\in\Omega} \lambda_k = 1, \tag{6.60}$$

where Sa and Dif are the sets of object pairs that belong to the same and different classes, respectively. Because this above objective is linear with respect to λ, a two-norm regularizer on the weighting vector λ can be further introduced to avoid overfitting. With the two-norm regularizer, the objective function can be rewritten as

$$\min_{\lambda} \sum_{(O_i,O_j)\in Sa} \sum_{k\in\Omega} D_{ij}^{(k)} - \sum_{(O_i,O_j)\in Dif} \sum_{k\in\Omega} D_{ij}^{(k)} + \mu\|\lambda\|^2$$

$$\text{s.t.} \quad \lambda_k \geq 0, \sum_{k\in\Omega} \lambda_k = 1. \tag{6.61}$$

The coordinate gradient descent approach can be used here to solve this optimization problem. During each iteration, two elements are updated and other elements are fixed in the same round. In one iteration, λ_u and λ_v can be updated and according to the constraint $\sum_{k\in\Omega} \lambda_k = 1$, $\lambda_u + \lambda_v$ will not change after this iteration. The updating rule can accordingly be written as

$$\begin{cases} \lambda_u^* = 0, \lambda_v^* = \lambda_u + \lambda_v, & \text{if} \quad 2\mu(\lambda_u + \lambda_v) + (b_v - b_u) \leq 0 \\ \lambda_u^* = \lambda_u + \lambda_v, \lambda_v^* = 0, & \text{if} \quad 2\mu(\lambda_u + \lambda_v) + (b_u - b_v) \leq 0 \\ \lambda_u^* = \dfrac{2\mu(\lambda_u + \lambda_v) + (b_v - b_u)}{4\mu}, \lambda_v^* = \lambda_u + \lambda_v - \lambda_u^*, & \text{otherwise,} \end{cases}$$

$$\tag{6.62}$$

where

$$b_u = \sum_{(O_i,O_j)\in Sa} D_{ij}^{(u)} - \sum_{(O_i,O_j)\in Dif} D_{ij}^{(u)} \tag{6.63}$$

and

$$b_v = \sum_{(O_i,O_j)\in Sa} D_{ij}^{(v)} - \sum_{(O_i,O_j)\in Dif} D_{ij}^{(v)}. \qquad (6.64)$$

It is noticed that each iteration cannot increase the objective function values. Thus, the convergence of the iteration process can be guaranteed.

An advantage of the GMM model in V3DOR is its robustness with respect to the unfixed multiple views for different objects. The multiple GMMs with learned weights can explore the structure better for V3DOR.

6.5 SUMMARY

In this chapter, we briefly reviewed existing multiple-view distance metrics for 3DOR, including the fundamental many-to-many distance measures, bipartite graph matching, and statistical matching methods. We note that measuring the distance between two groups of views for 3-D objects is difficult because of the complex relationship among multiple views. Although extensive research efforts have been dedicated to pairwise object matching, many challenging tasks remain. First, the distance metric for view matching is not well defined. Determining an optimal distance metric should be explored further. Second, the multiple-view feature modeling is still not accurate. The GMM-based method has been shown to be superior in 3DOR, while additional work is still required to narrow the semantic gap in 3DOR.

REFERENCES

[1] Atallah MJ. A linear time algorithm for the Hausdorff distance between convex polygons. Inf Process Lett 1983;17:207-9.

[2] Dubuisson MP, Jain AK. Modified Hausdorff distance for object matching. In: Proceedings of the IAPR International Conference on Pattern Recognition; 1994. p. 566-8.

[3] Daras P, Axenopoulos A. A 3D shape retrieval framework supporting multimodal queries. Int J Comput Vis 2010;89(2):229-47.

[4] Shih JL, Lee CH, Wang JT. A new 3D model retrieval approach based on the elevation descriptor. Pattern Recogn 2007;40:283-95.

[5] Gao Y, Dai Q, Wang M, Zhang N. 3D model retrieval using weighted bipartite graph matching. Signal Process Image Commun 2011;26(1):39-47.

[6] Ansary TF, Daoudi M, Vandeborre JP. A Bayesian 3D search engine using adaptive views clustering. IEEE Trans Multimed 2007;9(1):78-88.

[7] Gao Y, Tang J, Hong R, Yan S, Dai Q, Zhang N, Chua TS. Camera constraint-free view-based 3D object retrieval. IEEE Trans Image Process 2012;21(4):2269-81.

[8] Wang M, Gao Y, Lu K, Rui Y. View-based discriminative probabilistic modeling for 3D object retrieval and recognition. IEEE Trans Image Process 2013;22(4):1395-407.

[9] Xiao WS. Graph theory and its algorithms; 1993.

[10] Steinbach M, Karypis G, Kumar V. A comparison of document clustering techniques. In: KDD Workshop TextMining; 2000. p. 1-2.

[11] Khotanzad A, Hong YH. Invariant image recognition by Zernike moments. IEEE Trans Pattern Anal Mach Intell 1990;12(5):489-97.

[12] Yap PT, Paramesran R, Ong SH. Image analysis by Krawtchouk moments. IEEE Trans Image Process 2003;12(11):1367-77.

[13] Li F, Dai QH, Xu WL, Er GH. Statistical modeling and many-to-many matching for view-based 3D object retrieval. Signal Process Image Commun 2010;25(1):18-27.

[14] Kim WY, Kim YS. A region-based shape descriptor using Zernike moments. Signal Process Image Commun 2000;16(1-2):95-102.

[15] Li F, Dai Q, Xu WL, Er GH. Histogram mining based on Markov chain and its application to image categorization. Signal Process Image Commun 2007;22(9):785-96.

[16] Kullback S, Liebler R. On information and sufficiency. Ann Math Stat 1951;22:79-86.

[17] Bishop C, Nasser M. Pattern recognition and machine learning; 2006.

[18] Reynolds DA, Quatieri TF, Dunn RB. Speaker verification using adapted Gaussian mixture models. Digital Signal Process 2000;10(1):19-41.

[19] Zivkovic Z. Improved adaptive Gaussian mixture model for background subtraction. In: Proceedings of the 17th International Conference on Pattern Recognition, vol. 2; 2004. p. 28-31.

[20] KaewTraKulPong P, Bowden R. An improved adaptive background mixture model for real-time tracking with shadow detection. In: Video-Based Surveillance Systems; 2002. p. 135-44.

[21] Dempster A, Laird N, Rubin D. Maximum likelihood from incomplete data via the EM algorithm. J R Stat Soc Ser B 1977;39(1)1-38.

[22] Bishop CM. Pattern recognition and machine learning. New York: Springer; 2006.

[23] Lee C, Lin C, Juang B. A study on speaker adaptation of the parameters of continuous density hidden Markov models. IEEE Trans Signal Process 1994;39(4):806-14.

[24] Zhou X, Yan S, Chang SF, Hasegawa-Johnson M, Huang TS. SIFT-bag kernel for video event analysis. In: Proceedings of ACM International Conference on Multimedia; 2008.

[25] Zhuang X, Zhou X, Hasegawa-Johnson M, Huang TS. Face age estimation using patch-based hidden Markov model supervectors. In: Proceedings of International Conference on Pattern Recognition; 2008.

[26] Goldberger J, Roweis S, Hinton G, Salakhutdinov R. Neighborhood component analysis. In: Proceedings of Neural Information Processing Systems; 2004.

[27] Rissanen, J. Stochastic complexity in statistical inquiry theory. World Scientific Publishing Co., Inc., 1989.

CHAPTER 7

Learning-Based 3-D Object Retrieval

7.1 INTRODUCTION

In the last section, we introduced the multiple-view distance metrics, which are mainly based on pairwise object comparison. It is difficult to explore the relevance among multiple objects, although extensive research efforts have been dedicated to object matching methods in V3DOR. The relevance in 3-D objects generally contains not only pairwise similarity but also cross-object similarity, which takes all objects into account. Exploiting the underlying structure of 3-D objects is important for accurate 3DOR.

Rapid progress has been made in learning-based methods, particularly the semi-supervised learning (SSL) method [1]. SSL is a type of supervised learning method that employs not only the labeled samples for training but also the unlabeled data. Generally, the labeled data are very limited, while there is a large amount of unlabeled data for SSL tasks. By leveraging a large amount of unlabeled data based on certain assumptions, SSL methods are expected to build more accurate models than the models derived from purely supervised methods. Existing research has shown that a considerable improvement can be achieved when the unlabeled data are used in conjunction with the limited labeled samples, even with only a very small amount of labeled samples. As the annotation task may be laborious or infeasible, however, such as labeling all 3-D objects in a website or cataloging the 3-D structure of protein samples, the inexpensive unlabeled data can still be a good way to proceed.

Recently, graph-based SSL methods [2] that take advantage of the label smoothness assumption have been introduced by Seeger [3] and Chapelle et al. [4]. These methods define a graph where the vertices are both labeled and unlabeled samples and the edges reflect the similarities between the pairs. A labeling function is then estimated on the graph. The label smoothness over the graph is characterized in a regularization framework, which has a regularizer term and a loss function term. Graph-based SSL algorithms [5] have shown encouraging performance in many machine learning and data mining applications, especially when the labeled data are extremely few. A special type of graph-based learning method is hypergraph learning. Hypergraph learning [6] has been employed in many data mining and information retrieval tasks, such as image retrieval and object recognition. Zhou et al. [6] introduced a general hypergraph learning framework for data clustering, classification, and embedding. For image retrieval, Huang et al. [7] proposed a transductive learning framework in which an image hypergraph was constructed and each vertex in the hypergraph denoted one image. A unified hypergraph learning approach for music recommendation has also been proposed by Bu et al. [8].

Because of the advantages of SSL, this method has been investigated in V3DOR tasks, such as determining the optimal distance metric and object relevance. A Hausdorff distance metric learning method is introduced in Gao et al. [9], in which a view-level distance metric can be optimally defined by determining the object relevance to enhance the object-level Hausdorff distance measure. Under the bipartite graph matching framework, a bipartite graph optimal matching method is introduced in [10] to determine both the view-level distance metric and the object-level relevance among 3-D objects. Considering the high-order relevance among multiple views, a hypergraph-based learning method [11] is introduced to model 3-D objects in a hypergraph structure, in which view-level similarity is employed to construct the object hypergraph. All these methods follow SSL in leveraging the unlabeled data with very limited labeled 3-D objects, such as only the query object or just a very few labeled samples.

In this chapter, we first introduce the methods related to learning the optimal distance metric, followed by the hypergraph learning methods for 3-D object relevance estimation. We summarize this chapter in the last part.

7.2 LEARNING OPTIMAL DISTANCE METRICS

In this section, we introduce the learning methods for optimal distance metrics in V3DOR, including Hausdorff distance learning and bipartite graph optimal matching.

7.2.1 Hausdorff Distance Learning

Hausdorff distance [12, 13] has been introduced in the last section and we briefly review it here. We let O_1 and O_2 denote two compared 3-D objects with n_1 and n_2 views, respectively. d_v is the view-level distance and d_o is the object-level distance. $r(O_i)$ is the relationship of O to the query object.

By using the Mahalanobis distance metric $\mathbf{M}$, d_v between two views $\{v_i, v_j\}$ can be rewritten as

$$d_v(v_i, v_j) = (v_i - v_j)^T \mathbf{M}(v_i - v_j). \tag{7.1}$$

Then the Hausdorff distance between O_1 and O_2 can be rewritten as

$$d_o(O_1, O_2) = \max\{h(O_1, O_2), h(O_2, O_1)\}, \tag{7.2}$$

where $h(O_1, O_2)$ and $h(O_2, O_1)$ are defined by

$$h(O_1, O_2) = \max_{v_i \in O_1}\left\{\min_{v_j \in O_2}\{d_v(v_i, v_j)\}\right\} \tag{7.3}$$

and

$$h(O_2, O_1) = \max_{v_i \in O_2}\left\{\min_{v_j \in O_1}\{d_v(v_i, v_j)\}\right\}. \tag{7.4}$$

$d_o(O_1, O_2)$ can be further rewritten as

$$d_o(O_1, O_2) = \sum_{\substack{v_s \in O_1, \\ v_t \in O_2}} w_{ij}^{st} d_v(v_s, v_t), \tag{7.5}$$

where $w_{ij}^{st} = 1$ is for the view pair from the two compared objects that satisfies $d_v(v_s, v_t) = d_o(O_1, O_2)$. Otherwise $w_{ij}^{st} = 0$.

The relevance score of O_t to the query Q via kernel regression [14] based on the relevant sample set S_{pos} and the negative sample set S_{neg} is given by

$$r(O_t) = \frac{\sum_{O_i \in S_{pos}} \exp\left(-\frac{d_o(O_t,O_i)}{\sigma^2}\right) - \sum_{O_i \in S_{neg}} \exp\left(-\frac{d_o(O_t,O_i)}{\sigma^2}\right)}{\sum_{O_i \in \{S_{pos}, S_{neg}\}} \exp\left(-\frac{d_o(O_t,O_i)}{\sigma^2}\right)}, \tag{7.6}$$

where σ is the radius parameter in kernel regression.

As introduced in the definition, Hausdorff distance can determine the closest matching in all view pairs. However, Hausdorff distance is based on the view-level distance measure and generally the Euclidean distance is used to measure the view-level distance, which may be inappropriate. For example, there are typically some redundant features for multiple views, which may lead to incorrect matching between the two groups of views.

Distance metric learning algorithms have accordingly been investigated in recent years [15, 16] to produce a better pairwise distance measure. However, it is difficult to optimize Hausdorff distance in V3DOR because the label information is on the object level while the distance metric is based on view features.

To learn an optimal Hausdorff distance metric, we introduce an SSL method in [9]. In this method, the Hausdorff distances between the query object and other objects are calculated to return the initial retrieval results. With the user relevance feedback, the top results can be marked by the user as either positive or negative to the query. The Hausdorff distance metric is updated by determining the view-level distance metric. Then, the kernel regression method is adopted to rerank all 3-D objects with the goal of achieving optimal retrieval results. This process is repeated until satisfactory retrieval results are achieved. Figure 7.1 illustrates the framework of this method.

Here, the Zernike moments [17] are employed as the view feature. Given the query object Q, traditional Hausdorff distance is conducted to achieve the initial retrieval results, in which the view-level distance metric $\mathbf{M}$ is first initialed as $\mathbf{I}$. Then, the top results are shown to the user and the user can manually annotate the results as being either positive or negative samples. Here, we let S_{pos} and S_{neg} denote the positive and negative sample sets, respectively.

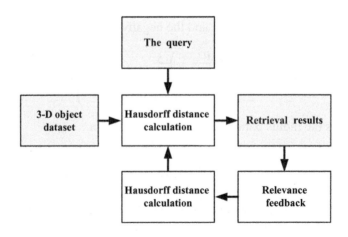

Figure 7.1 The framework of the Hausdorff distance learning method for 3DOR [9].

The objective is to learn an optimal distance metric $\mathbf{M}$ in the Hausdorff distance. A better $\mathbf{M}$ can make the query more discriminative. To this end, the distances between the objects in the same class should be minimized and the distances of the objects from the different classes should be constrained as

$$F = \sum_{O_i, O_j \in S_{pos}} d_o \left(O_i, O_j \right)$$

$$\text{s.t.} \quad \sum_{\substack{O_i \in S_{pos}, \\ O_j \in S_{neg}}} d_o \left(O_i, O_j \right) \geq 1. \tag{7.7}$$

This expression can also be rewritten to involve Hausdorff distance according to

$$F = \sum_{O_i, O_j \in S_{pos}} \sum_{\substack{v_s \in O_i, \\ v_t \in O_j}} w_{ij}^{st} d_v \left(v_s, v_t \right)$$

$$= \sum_{O_i, O_j \in S_{pos}} \sum_{\substack{v_s \in O_i, \\ v_t \in O_j}} w_{ij}^{st} (v_s - v_t)^T \mathbf{M} (v_s - v_t)$$

$$\text{s.t.} \quad \sum_{\substack{O_i \in S_{pos}, \\ O_j \in S_{neg}}} \sum_{\substack{v_s \in O_i, \\ v_t \in O_j}} w_{ij}^{st} (v_s - v_t)^T \mathbf{M} (v_s - v_t) \geq 1, \tag{7.8}$$

where $\mathbf{M} \succ 0$, $w_{ij}^{st} = 1$ indicates that v_s and v_t are the selected pair of views from O_i and O_j for Hausdorff distance (as shown in the definition of Hausdorff distance), and $w_{ij}^{st} = 0$ indicates v_s and v_t are not the selected pair of views.

It is noted that it is a 0-1 programming task to solve the above optimization problem, which is computationally intractable. To handle this problem, a probabilistic view pair selection method is introduced to iteratively select the training view pairs, and the distance metric $\mathbf{M}$ can be iteratively updated.

Given the training samples S_{pos} and S_{neg}, a view pair is probabilistically selected, where either both views are from S_{pos} or one view is from S_{pos} and the other is from S_{neg}. These data are used to generate the training view pair samples.

Given an object pair, the closest view from the object is calculated for each view and one view pair is probabilistically selected by letting the view pair with the larger distance have a higher probability of being selected. Here, $\{v_1^1, v_2^1, \ldots, v_{n_1}^1\}$ and $\{v_1^2, v_2^2, \ldots, v_{n_2}^2\}$ denote views from O_1 and O_2, respectively. For each view $v_{s(s=1,2,\ldots,n_1)} \in O_1$, a view $v'_{s(s=1,2,\ldots,n_1)} \in O_2$ is selected that satisfies the following equation

$$v_s' = \arg \min_{v_i \in O_2} (d_v(v_s, v_i)), \tag{7.9}$$

where $\{v_s, v_s'\}$ is set as the sth candidate training view pair. For each view $v_{t(t=1,2,\ldots,n_2)} \in O_2$, a view $v'_{t(t=1,2,\ldots,n_2)} \in O_1$ is selected that satisfies $v_t' = \arg \min_{v_i \in O_1} (d_v(v_t, v_i))$. The view pair $\{v_t, v_t'\}$ is employed as the $(t + n_1)$th candidate training view pair.

Here, $n_1 + n_2$ candidate training view pairs are obtained, and the selection probabilities for all candidate training view pairs are calculated according to

$$P(\{v_k, v_k'\}) = \frac{1 - \exp\left(-\frac{d_v(v_k, v_k')}{\sigma^2}\right)}{\sum_{i=1}^{n_1+n_2}\left(1 - \exp\left(-\frac{d_v(v_i, v_i')}{\sigma^2}\right)\right)}, \quad k = 1, 2, \ldots, n_1 + n_2. \tag{7.10}$$

A view pair can be selected from these candidates based on these selection probabilities.

It is simple to determine that only one w_{ij}^{st} is 1 for all view pairs in an object pair and that all other w_{ij}^{st} values are 0, because only one view is the closest view for a given view. Then, the optimization task is changed to a standard distance metric learning task as introduced in Xing et al. [15]. In this way, the optimization task is first changed to

$$\max g(\mathbf{M}) = \max \sum_{\substack{O_i \in S_{pos}, \\ O_j \in S_{neg}}} \sum_{\substack{v_s \in O_i, \\ v_t \in O_j}} w_{ij}^{st} d_v(v_s, v_t)$$

$$\text{s.t.} \quad \sum_{\substack{O_i, O_j \in S_{pos}}} \sum_{\substack{v_s \in O_i, \\ v_t \in O_j}} w_{ij}^{st} d_v(v_s, v_t) \leq 1. \tag{7.11}$$

To determine the optimization results, the gradient descent method can be used here to iteratively optimize the objective function according to

$$\nabla_{\mathbf{M}} g(\mathbf{M}) = \sum_{\substack{O_i \in S_{pos}, \\ O_j \in S_{neg}}} \sum_{\substack{v_s \in O_i, \\ v_t \in O_j}} w_{ij}^{st} (v_s - v_t)(v_s - v_t)^T. \tag{7.12}$$

Then, the gradient descent iterative procedure is repeated as

$$\mathbf{M} := \mathbf{M} + \alpha \nabla_{\mathbf{M}} g(\mathbf{M}). \tag{7.13}$$

In each iteration round, if the objective function decreases, the distance metric $\mathbf{M}$ will be updated using the new one $\overline{\mathbf{M}}$. Otherwise, no action is conducted. This iterative process continues until the maximal number of loops is achieved. It has been shown that this iterative process is convergent. A detailed proof of convergence can be found in [9].

In this method, the computational cost is composed of the training view selection step and the view-level metric learning step. In the first step, the computational cost scales as $O(n_v^2(n_p(n_p + n_n)d_f^2))$. In the second step, the computation cost scales as $O((n_p + n_n)^2 d_f^2 + d_f^3)$, where n_v is the number of views for each object, d_f is the dimensionality of the employed feature, and n_p and n_n are the numbers of the positive and negative samples, respectively. Then, the computational cost of the entire method scales as $O(T(n_v^2(n_p(n_p + n_n)d_f^2) + (n_p + n_n)^2 d_f^2 + d_f^3))$, where T is the maximum iteration time.

7.2.2 Learning Bipartite Graph Optimal Matching

The bipartite graph has been employed in view-based 3-D object retrieval in Gao et al. [18], in which two sets of multiple views are formulated in a bipartite graph structure, and the optimal matching is conducted in the bipartite graph to measure the distance between two 3-D objects. To leverage both the unlabeled and labeled data, that is, the query object and/or labeled data from user relevance feedback, a graph-based SSL process is introduced to formulate the relationship among 3-D objects. This SSL process aims to explore the underlying structure of all 3-D objects with the goal of achieving better retrieval performance. A learning-based bipartite graph matching method is introduced in [10] to conduct V3DOR. Figure 7.2 illustrates the framework of this method, including bipartite graph matching, graph structure, and alternating optimization.

In this method, the Zernike moments [17] are extracted as the view feature. Given two sets of multiple views from two 3-D objects, O_1 and O_2, representative views are first generated by conducting the HAC method [19]. Generally, 5–15 view clusters are obtained for one 3-D object, which is similar to other works.

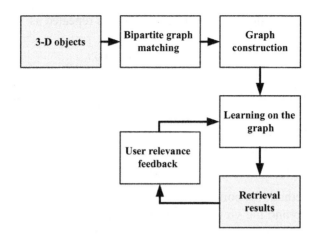

Figure 7.2 The framework of the bipartite graph learning method for 3DOR.

For object O_1, n_1 views $V_1 = \{v_{11}, v_{12}, \ldots, v_{1n_1}\}$ are selected with corresponding weights $P_1 = \{p_{11}, p_{12}, \ldots, p_{1n_1}\}$. For the other object O_2, representative views $V_2 = \{v_{21}, v_{22}, \ldots, v_{2n_2}\}$ and the weights $P_2 = \{p_{21}, p_{22}, \ldots, p_{2n_2}\}$ can be obtained in the same way.

A bipartite graph $G_b = \{V_1, V_2, E_b\}$ can next be constructed. In G_b, each vertex denotes one view O_1 or O_2 and the edge $E_b = \{e_{ij}\}$ is defined as

$$e_{ij} = -d\left(v_{1i}, v_{2j}\right) = -\left(f_{1i} - f_{2j}\right)^T \Lambda \left(f_{1i} - f_{2j}\right), \qquad (7.14)$$

where f_{1i} is the feature vector for v_{1i} and Λ is the distance metric for pairwise view comparison initialized by the identity matrix $\mathbf{I}$. Then, optimal matching on the bipartite graph is conducted to measure the distance between O_1 and O_2, which can be written as

$$d\left(O_1, O_2\right) = \sum_{i=1}^{n_1} d\left(v_{1i}, v_{2i}^{\times}\right) = \sum_{i=1}^{n_1} \left(f_{1i} - f_{2i}^{\times}\right)^T \Lambda \left(f_{1i} - f_{2i}^{\times}\right). \qquad (7.15)$$

Letting $\Lambda = \mathbf{M}^T \mathbf{M}$, we can derive

$$d\left(O_1, O_2\right) = \sum_{i=1}^{n_1} \left(f_{1i} - f_{2i}^{\times}\right)^T \mathbf{M}^T \mathbf{M} \left(f_{1i} - f_{2i}^{\times}\right). \qquad (7.16)$$

Here, the task is to infer the optimal correspondence of $f_{2i}^{\times}$ and the optimal distance metric $\mathbf{M}$. With the bipartite graph matching-based distance measure, the SSL framework [2] can be employed here to explore the global consistency among all 3-D objects. An object graph $G = (\mathbf{U}, \mathbf{E}, \mathbf{W})$ is constructed to formulate all 3-D objects, in which each vertex u_i represents one 3-D object and $\mathbf{E}$ is the edge linking all vertices. $\mathbf{W}$ is the $n \times n$ affinity matrix defined by

$$
\mathbf{W}(u_s, u_t) = \exp\left(-d\left(O_s, O_t\right)\right)
$$

$$
= \exp\left(-\sum_{i=1}^{n_s} \left(f_{si} - f_{ti}^{\times}\right)^T \mathbf{M}^T \mathbf{M} \left(f_{si} - f_{ti}^{\times}\right)\right). \tag{7.17}
$$

The diagonal matrix $\mathbf{D}$ reflects the edge degree, which is obtained by

$$
\mathbf{D}_{ss} = \sum_t \mathbf{W}(u_s, u_t). \tag{7.18}
$$

Here, each entry, $\mathbf{W}_{ij}$, represents the confidence score between two vertices.

The learning process on the object graph aims to jointly minimize the empirical loss and the graph regularizer, which can be written as

$$
\arg\min_{\mathbf{M},\mathbf{F}} \Gamma = \arg\min_{\mathbf{M},\mathbf{F}} \sum_{i,j=1}^{n} \mathbf{W}_{ij} \left\| \frac{\mathbf{F}_i}{\sqrt{\mathbf{D}_{ii}}} - \frac{\mathbf{F}_j}{\sqrt{\mathbf{D}_{jj}}} \right\|^2 + \mu \sum_{i=1}^{n} \|\mathbf{F}_i - \mathbf{Y}_i\|^2,
$$

$$
\tag{7.19}
$$

where $\mathbf{F}$ is the $n \times 1$ relevance vector to be determined, $\mathbf{Y}$ is the labeled data, the first term is the graph regularizer, and the second term is the empirical loss. The labeled data $\mathbf{Y}$ are generated as follows. In the first round of retrieval, $\mathbf{Y}$ is initialized by an $n \times 1$ matrix with zeros in all cells except the query with 1, because only that query is a labeled sample. In the following rounds of retrieval, $\mathbf{Y}$ can be labeled using the user relevance feedback, that is, 1 for positive samples and -1 for negative samples.

The above optimization task can be alternately solved. In the first step, $\mathbf{M}$ is fixed and $\mathbf{F}$ is optimized. The objective function reduces to

$$
\min_{\mathbf{F}} \sum_{i,j=1}^{n} \mathbf{W}_{ij} \left\| \frac{\mathbf{F}_i}{\sqrt{\mathbf{D}_{ii}}} - \frac{\mathbf{F}_j}{\sqrt{\mathbf{D}_{jj}}} \right\|^2 + \mu \sum_{i=1}^{n} \|\mathbf{F}_i - \mathbf{Y}_i\|^2. \tag{7.20}
$$

This optimization task can be solved by

$$\mathbf{F} = \left(\mathbf{I} + \frac{1}{\mu}\Delta\right)^{-1}\mathbf{Y}, \tag{7.21}$$

where $\Delta = \mathbf{D}^{-(1/2)}\mathbf{W}\mathbf{D}^{-(1/2)}$.

In the second step, $\mathbf{F}$ is fixed and $\mathbf{M}$ is optimized. The objective function reduces to

$$\min_{\mathbf{M}} \sum_{i,j,=1}^{n} \mathbf{W}_{ij} \left\| \frac{\mathbf{F}_i}{\sqrt{\mathbf{D}_{ii}}} - \frac{\mathbf{F}_j}{\sqrt{\mathbf{D}_{jj}}} \right\|^2. \tag{7.22}$$

Letting $\Psi = \sum_{i,j,=1}^{n} \mathbf{W}_{ij} \left\| \frac{\mathbf{F}_i}{\sqrt{\mathbf{D}_{ii}}} - \frac{\mathbf{F}_j}{\sqrt{\mathbf{D}_{jj}}} \right\|^2$, the derivation can be calculated by

$$\frac{\partial \sum_{i,j,=1}^{n} \mathbf{W}_{ij} \left\| \frac{\mathbf{F}_i}{\sqrt{\mathbf{D}_{ii}}} - \frac{\mathbf{F}_j}{\sqrt{\mathbf{D}_{jj}}} \right\|^2}{\partial \mathbf{M}}$$

$$= \sum_{i,j,=1}^{n} \left\{ \frac{\partial \sum_{i,j,=1}^{n} \mathbf{W}_{ij}}{\partial M} \left\| \frac{\mathbf{F}_i}{\sqrt{\mathbf{D}_{ii}}} - \frac{\mathbf{F}_j}{\sqrt{\mathbf{D}_{jj}}} \right\|^2 \right.$$

$$\left. - \mathbf{W}_{ij} \left(\frac{\left(\frac{\mathbf{F}_i}{\sqrt{\mathbf{D}_{ii}}} - \frac{\mathbf{F}_j}{\sqrt{\mathbf{D}_{jj}}}\right)^T \mathbf{F}_i}{\sqrt{\mathbf{D}_{ii}^3}} \frac{\partial \mathbf{D}_{ii}}{\partial \mathbf{M}} - \frac{\left(\frac{\mathbf{F}_i}{\sqrt{\mathbf{D}_{ii}}} - \frac{\mathbf{F}_j}{\sqrt{\mathbf{D}_{jj}}}\right)^T \mathbf{F}_j}{\sqrt{\mathbf{D}_{jj}^3}} \frac{\partial \mathbf{D}_{jj}}{\partial \mathbf{M}} \right) \right\}, \tag{7.23}$$

where

$$\frac{\partial \mathbf{D}_{ii}}{\partial \mathbf{M}} = \sum_{j=1}^{n} \frac{\partial \mathbf{W}_{ij}}{\partial \mathbf{M}} \tag{7.24}$$

and

$$\frac{\partial \mathbf{W}_{ij}}{\partial \mathbf{M}} = -2\mathbf{W}_{ij}\mathbf{M} \sum_{s=1}^{n_i} \left(f_{is} - f_{is}^{\times}\right)^T \left(f_{is} - f_{is}^{\times}\right). \tag{7.25}$$

Here, $\mathbf{M}$ can be updated using the gradient descent algorithm

$$\mathbf{M}_{k+1} = \mathbf{M}_k - \alpha \frac{\partial \Psi}{\partial \mathbf{M}}. \qquad (7.26)$$

In this process, the corresponding view feature $f_{is}^{\times}$ for f_{is} is determined in the bipartite graph matching step. In each iteration round, an updated distance metric $\mathbf{M}$ can be used in the next iteration of bipartite graph matching, which can further lead to new $f_{is}^{\times}$ values for each f_{is}.

The 3DOR process can be summarized as follows. Given a query object, bipartite graph matching is conducted to calculate the object pairwise distances. Then, we conduct SSL to generate $\mathbf{F}$ to rerank these objects. Using the top labeled results, both $\mathbf{M}$ and $\mathbf{F}$ are iteratively updated and we obtain the new object pairwise distances. This process is repeated until satisfactory results are achieved.

In this method, the bipartite graph matching costs $O(\bar{n}_v^3)$, where $\bar{n}_v$ is the number of views for each object. The graph construction costs $O(n^2)$, where n is the number of objects. The computational cost for the SSL and metric update is $O(T_1 T_2 n^3)$, where T_1 and T_2 are the numbers of maximal iterations in the two learning procedures.

The merit of this method lies in its ability to jointly learn the pairwise object distance metric and the global consistency among 3-D objects.

7.3 3-D OBJECT RELEVANCE ESTIMATION VIA HYPERGRAPH LEARNING

Generally, the major difference between image retrieval and V3DOR lies in the multiple views of 3-D object representation, which lead to higher-order information in 3-D objects compared with single images. Although existing matching methods, such as Hausdorff distance, EMD, bipartite graph matching, and probabilistic methods, have made significant achievements in the realm of multiple views, they still have limitations related to modeling the high-order relationship among multiple views of 3-D objects.

Recent studies of hypergraphs have been superior at modeling high-order information. Because of this advantage, we propose a hypergraph-based 3-D object relevance estimation method in [11], in which the relationship among 3-D objects is formulated based on a hypergraph structure. In this section, we first introduce the basic concept of hypergraphs and their applications. Next, we introduce the hypergraph-based 3DOR methods.

7.3.1 Hypergraph and Its Applications

A hypergraph is a generalization of a graph in which each edge can connect any number of vertices, instead of only two vertices, as in a simple graph. Figures 7.3 and 7.4 show examples of a simple graph and a hypergraph, respectively.

In a hypergraph $G = (\mathbf{V}, \mathbf{E})$, $\mathbf{V}$ is the vertex set and $\mathbf{E}$ is the edge set. For a weighted hypergraph $G = (\mathbf{V}, \mathbf{E}, w)$, w is the weight for the edges. An incidence matrix $\mathbf{H}$ is associated with G, which is a $|\mathbf{V}| \times |\mathbf{E}|$ matrix defined as

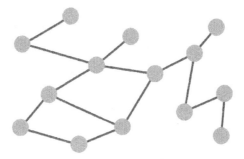

Figure 7.3 An example of the simple graph.

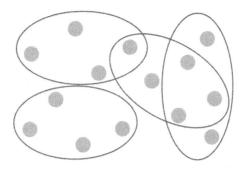

Figure 7.4 An example of the hypergraph.

$$h(v, e) = \begin{cases} 1 & \text{if } v \in e \\ 0 & \text{if } v \notin e \end{cases}. \tag{7.27}$$

For a weighted hypergraph $G = (\mathbf{V}, \mathbf{E}, w)$, the vertex degree for a vertex $v \in \mathbf{V}$ is defined as

$$d(v) = \sum_{e \in \mathbf{E}} \omega(e) h(v, e). \tag{7.28}$$

The edge degree for an edge $e \in \mathbf{E}$ is defined as

$$\delta(e) = \sum_{v \in \mathbf{V}} h(v, e). \tag{7.29}$$

The vertex degrees and the edge degrees can be represented by two diagonal matrices $\mathbf{D}_v$ and $\mathbf{D}_e$, in which each diagonal entry denotes one vertex degree or edge degree. A diagonal matrix $\mathbf{W}$ denotes the edge weights.

In recent years, hypergraph-based SSL [6] has been thoroughly investigated in many applications. Different learning tasks can be conducted in the hypergraph structure to learn the optimal relationship, classification, clustering, ranking, and embedding [6, 20–22]. To match two sets of features, a probabilistic hypergraph is conducted and the matching is performed in the hypergraph structure [23]. In image retrieval, a joint hypergraph, which is generated using both the visual content and the social tags, is constructed and learning on the hypergraph is used to rank the images [24, 25]. In a study by Huang et al. [7], a transductive learning framework is introduced for image retrieval, in which each vertex denotes one image. The probabilistic hypergraph is constructed using the similarity among images. For object classification [26], both local SIFT and global geometric constraints are integrated into a class-specific hypergraph to learn the object classification with multiple appearances. An extension toward a large-scale class-specific hypergraph model is introduced in a study by Xia and Hancock [27]. Hypergraphs have been employed for 3-D object representation. In an analysis by Wong and Lu [28], a hypergraph is constructed using the correlation among different surface boundary segments of an object from the computer-aided design (CAD) system. In the CAD system, each 3-D model is composed of multiple surface patches and each distinct surface patch is regarded as a surface boundary segment.

In the hypergraph, each vertex denotes one boundary segment and the corresponding length and angle between adjacent segments are employed as the associated attributes. The edge is calculated as the connection between two segments.

As introduced in Zhou et al. [6], the general binary classification task can be performed in the following regularization framework:

$$\arg\min_{f}\left\{\lambda R_{\text{emp}}(f) + \Omega(f)\right\},\tag{7.30}$$

where f is the target classification function, $\Omega(f)$ is a regularizer on the hypergraph structure, $R_{\text{emp}}(f)$ is an empirical loss, and $\lambda > 0$ is the trade-off parameter.

Here, the hypergraph regularizer can be defined as

$$\Omega(f) = \frac{1}{2}\sum_{e\in\mathbf{E}}\sum_{u,v\in\mathbf{V}}\frac{w(e)\,h(u,e)\,h(v,e)}{\delta(e)}\left(\frac{f(u)}{\sqrt{d(u)}} - \frac{f(v)}{\sqrt{d(v)}}\right)^2.\tag{7.31}$$

Letting $\Theta = \mathbf{D}_v^{-(1/2)}\mathbf{HWD}_e^{-1}\mathbf{H}^T\mathbf{D}_v^{-(1/2)}$, and $\Delta = \mathbf{I} - \Theta$, the normalized cost function can be rewritten as

$$\Omega(f) = f^T\Delta f,\tag{7.32}$$

where Δ is a positive semidefinite matrix, called the hypergraph Laplacian.

7.3.2 Learning on Single Hypergraph

Because of the superiority of high-order information modeling, hypergraphs have been introduced in V3DOR [11], in which the relationship among 3-D objects is formulated in a hypergraph structure. Figure 7.5 illustrates the algorithm, including two main steps: hypergraph construction and learning on the hypergraph.

In this first step, an object hypergraph is constructed by exploring the view-level relevance among different 3-D objects. To construct the object hypergraph, each 3-D object in the data set is denoted by a vertex in a weighted hypergraph $G = (\mathbf{V}, \mathbf{E}, w)$. Assuming that there are n objects in the data set, the hypergraph G that is generated has n vertices. The connection (edge) among these vertices is generated using a view-clustering method. All the views of these 3-D objects are grouped into clusters using the K-means algorithm [29] and each view cluster is regarded as one edge in the

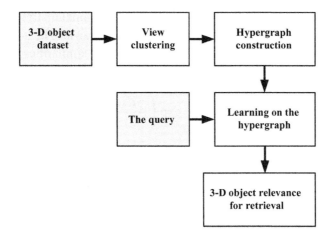

Figure 7.5 The framework of hypergraph learning in 3DOR [11].

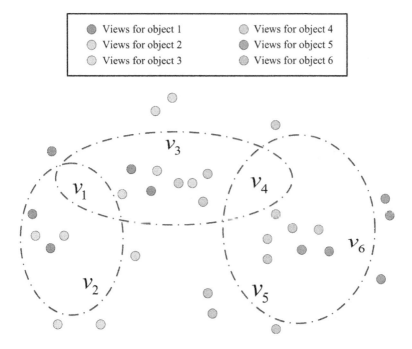

Figure 7.6 Illustration of the hypergraph edge generation method.

object hypergraph G. The 3-D objects that have views in the same view cluster are connected by a corresponding edge, leading to an edge in the hypergraph for each view cluster. Figure 7.6 shows a schematic illustration of the proposed hypergraph edge generation method.

An incidence matrix $\mathbf{H}$ is generated for G. Diagonal matrices $\mathbf{D}_v$ and $\mathbf{D}_e$ for vertex degrees and edge degrees, respectively, can also be generated. The edge weight w can be calculated by the sum of the similarities between two vertices in the cluster, that is,

$$w(e) = \sum_{x_a, x_b \in e} \exp\left(-\frac{d(x_a, x_b)^2}{\sigma^2}\right), \tag{7.33}$$

where x_a and x_b are two views in the same cluster and $d(x_a, x_b)$ is the distance between these two views. σ can be empirically set to the median value of the distances of all view pairs. By using this hypergraph construction method, two objects tend to be connected by more edges if they share more similar views, and an edge can be assigned a higher weight if the views in the corresponding view cluster are more similar.

Given the object hypergraph $G = (\mathbf{V}, \mathbf{E}, w)$, 3DOR can be regarded as a one-class classification task [7], in which the query object is the only positive sample for the target class. The one-class classification task can be formulated in the following regularization framework:

$$\arg\min_f \{\lambda R_{\text{emp}}(f) + \Omega(f)\}, \tag{7.34}$$

where the hypergraph regularizer term $\Omega(f)$ is defined by

$$\frac{1}{2}\sum_{e \in E}\sum_{u,v \in V} \frac{w(e)\,h(u,e)\,h(v,e)}{\delta(e)}\left(\frac{f(u)}{\sqrt{d(u)}} - \frac{f(v)}{\sqrt{d(v)}}\right)^2, \tag{7.35}$$

where the vector f is the relevance score vector to be learned. (Eq. (7.35)) further turns to

$$\Omega(f) = \sum_{e \in E}\sum_{u,v \in V} \frac{w(e)\,h(u,e)\,h(v,e)}{\delta(e)}\left(\frac{f^2(u)}{d(u)} - \frac{f(u)f(v)}{\sqrt{d(u)\,d(v)}}\right)$$

$$= \left\{\sum_{u \in V} f^2(u)\sum_{e \in E}\frac{w_i(e)\,h(u,e)}{d(u)}\sum_{v \in V}\frac{h(v,e)}{\delta(e)}\right.$$

$$\left. - \sum_{e \in E}\sum_{u,v \in V}\frac{f(u)h(u,e)\,w(e)\,h(v,e)f(v)}{\sqrt{d(u)\,d(v)}\delta(e)}\right\}$$

$$= f^T(\mathbf{I} - \Theta)f, \tag{7.36}$$

where $\Theta = \mathbf{D}_v^{-(1/2)}\mathbf{H}\mathbf{W}\mathbf{D}_e^{-1}\mathbf{H}^T\mathbf{D}_v^{-(1/2)}$. Let $\Delta\mathbf{I} - \Theta$. The term Δ can be viewed as the hypergraph Laplacian. Thus, we obtain

$$\Omega(f) = f^T\Delta f. \tag{7.37}$$

The loss function term is defined according to

$$\|f - y\|^2 = \sum_{u \in V}(f(u) - y(u))^2, \tag{7.38}$$

where y is the $n \times 1$ labeled vector. In the retrieval task, only the query entry is 1 and all other elements are 0. The learning task for 3DOR becomes minimizing the sum of the two terms according to

$$\Phi(f) = f^T\Delta f + \lambda\|f - y\|^2, \tag{7.39}$$

where $\lambda > 0$ is the weighting parameter.

To solve this problem, differentiating $\Phi(f)$ with respect to f, we obtain

$$f = \left(\mathbf{I} + \frac{1}{\lambda}\Delta\right)^{-1}y. \tag{7.40}$$

According to a study by Zhou et al. [2], the problem can be efficiently solved by an iterative process as

$$f^{(t+1)} = \frac{1}{1+\lambda}(\mathbf{I} - \Delta)f^{(t)} + \frac{\lambda}{1+\lambda}y. \tag{7.41}$$

The convergence of this iterative process can be proved as follows. Because $\Theta = \mathbf{D}_v^{-(1/2)}\mathbf{H}\mathbf{W}\mathbf{D}_e^{-1}\mathbf{H}^T\mathbf{D}_v^{-(1/2)}$, we derive that its eigenvalues are in $[-1, 1]$. Therefore, $(\mathbf{I} \pm \Theta)$ are positive semidefinite, which means that the eigenvalues of Θ are in $[-1, 1]$.

Without any loss of generality, suppose $f^{(0)} = y$. From the iterative process, we have

$$f^{(t)} = \left(\frac{\lambda}{1+\lambda}\right)\sum_{i=0}^{t-1}\left(\frac{1}{1+\lambda}\Theta\right)^i y + \left(\frac{1}{1+\lambda}\Theta\right)^t y$$

$$= (1 - \zeta)\sum_{i=0}^{t-1}(\zeta\Theta)^i y + (\zeta\Theta)^t y, \tag{7.42}$$

where $\zeta = \frac{1}{1+\lambda}$.

Because $0 < \zeta < 1$ and the eigenvalues of Θ are in $[-1, 1]$, we derive that

$$\lim_{t \to \infty} (\zeta\Theta)^t = 0 \tag{7.43}$$

and

$$\lim_{t \to \infty} \sum_{i=0}^{t-1} (\zeta\Theta)^i = (\mathbf{I} - \zeta\Theta)^{-1}. \tag{7.44}$$

Therefore, we obtain

$$f = \lim_{t \to \infty} f^{(t)} = (1 - \zeta)(\mathbf{I} - \zeta\Theta)^{-1} y = \left(\mathbf{I} + \frac{1}{\lambda}\Delta\right)^{-1} y, \tag{7.45}$$

which completes the proof.

With the learned relevance vector f, which indicates the relevance scores of each object to the query, all objects can be ranked in descending order to generate the 3DOR results. In this method, the view-level relevance can be represented in a hypergraph structure, which can explore the high-order information beyond the pairwise view relationship.

7.3.3 Learning on Multiple Hypergraphs

The constructed hypergraph determines the performance of the object relevance estimation. A poorly generated hypergraph structure will lead to unsatisfactory 3DOR results because the structure cannot reflect the object relationship well. Therefore, constructing a well-designed hypergraph is an important task in this method. As introduced previously, the object hypergraph is constructed using view clustering, while it is difficult to produce a good clustering result. The edge generated with the K-means clustering method is significantly influenced by parameter K, which controls the number of generated edges. Selecting parameter K is challenging. A smaller K value may lead to a poorer discriminative ability but a larger K value can split the object relationship too much.

To address this problem, we further propose a multiple hypergraph-based learning method in [11], in which multiple K-means clustering procedures are used with respect to different K values. Figure 7.7 illustrates the framework of the multiple hypergraph learning method for 3DOR.

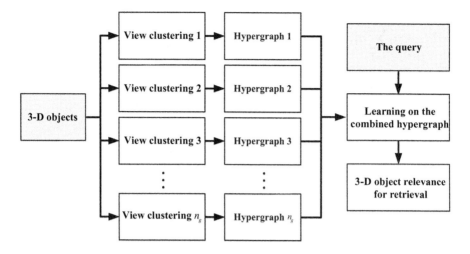

Figure 7.7 The framework of the multiple hypergraph learning method for 3DOR [11].

In this method, different hypergraphs can be constructed in the view clustering step by varying the number of generated clusters. These hypergraphs can represent the relationship among these views in different granularities. As discussed above, some edges can reflect the true relationship well while others may not. Therefore, combining these hypergraphs to conduct hypergraph learning is important for optimal 3-D object relevance estimation. Here, let $G_1 = (\mathbf{V}_1, \mathbf{E}_1, w_1)$, $G_2 = (\mathbf{V}_2, \mathbf{E}_2, w_2)$, ..., and $G_{n_g} = (\mathbf{V}_{n_g}, \mathbf{E}_{n_g}, w_{n_g})$ denote the n_g hypergraphs with different granularities. For these n_g hypergraphs, n_g incidence matrices, vertex degree matrices, and edge degree matrices, that is, $\{\mathbf{H}_1, \mathbf{H}_2, \ldots, \mathbf{H}_{n_g}\}$, $\{\mathbf{D}_{v1}, \mathbf{D}_{v2}, \ldots, \mathbf{D}_{vn_g}\}$, and $\{\mathbf{D}_{e1}, \mathbf{D}_{e2}, \ldots, \mathbf{D}_{en_g}\}$, are generated, respectively. Here, let u_i denote the weight of the ith hypergraph, where $\sum_{i=1}^{n_g} \alpha_i = 1$, and $\alpha_i \geq 0$. α_i can be first initialed as $\frac{1}{n_g}$.

Following the previous learning framework, the hypergraph regularizer $\Omega(f)$ in the objective function $\arg\min_f \{\lambda R_{emp}(f) + \Omega(f)\}$ can be rewritten as

$$\Omega(f) = \frac{1}{2} \sum_{i=1}^{n_g} \alpha_i \sum_{e \in \mathbf{E}_i} \sum_{u,v \in \mathbf{V}_i} \frac{w_i(e) h_i(u,e) h_i(v,e)}{\delta_i(e)} \left(\frac{f(u)}{\sqrt{d_i(u)}} - \frac{f(v)}{\sqrt{d_i(v)}} \right)^2$$

$$= \sum_{i=1}^{n_g} \alpha_i \sum_{e \in \mathbf{E}_i} \sum_{u,v \in \mathbf{V}_i} \frac{w_i(e) h_i(u,e) h_i(v,e)}{\delta_i(e)} \left(\frac{f^2(u)}{d_i(u)} - \frac{f(u) f(v)}{\sqrt{d_i(u) d_i(v)}} \right)$$

$$
= \sum_{i=1}^{n_g} \alpha_i \left\{ \sum_{u \in \mathbf{V}_i} f^2 (u) \sum_{e \in \mathbf{E}_i} \frac{w_i (e) h_i (u, e)}{d_i (u)} \sum_{v \in \mathbf{V}_i} \frac{h_i (v, e)}{\delta_i (e)} \right.
$$

$$
\left. - \sum_{e \in \mathbf{E}_i} \sum_{u, v \in \mathbf{V}_i} \frac{f(u) h_i (u, e) w_i (e) h_i (v, e) f(v)}{\sqrt{d_i (u) d_i (v)} \delta_i (e)} \right\}
$$

$$
= \sum_{i=1}^{n_g} \alpha_i f^T (\mathbf{I} - \Theta_i) f
$$

$$
= f^T \sum_{i=1}^{n_g} \alpha_i (\mathbf{I} - \Theta_i) f
$$

$$
= f^T \Delta f, \tag{7.46}
$$

where $\Theta_i = \mathbf{D}_{vi}^{-(1/2)} \mathbf{H}_i \mathbf{W}_i \mathbf{D}_{ei}^{-1} \mathbf{H}_i^T \mathbf{D}_{vi}^{-(1/2)}$. Let $\Delta = \sum_{i=1}^{n_g} \alpha_i (\mathbf{I} - \Theta_i) = \mathbf{I} - \sum_{i=1}^{n_g} \alpha_i \Theta_i = \mathbf{I} - \Theta$, where $\Theta = \sum_{i=1}^{n_g} \alpha_i \Theta_i$.

As shown in (Eq. (7.46)), the multiple hypergraphs can be combined in the learning process as the hypergraph regularizer. The Δ term can be regarded as the multiple hypergraph Laplacian. A similar solution can be achieved by

$$
f = \left(\mathbf{I} + \frac{1}{\lambda} \Delta \right)^{-1} y. \tag{7.47}
$$

7.3.4 Learning the Weights for Multiple Hypergraphs

In the last part all hypergraphs are given equal weights, that is, $\frac{1}{n_g}$. It is noted that these multiple hypergraphs with different granularities may have different effects on 3-D object relationship modeling. Therefore, learning an optimal weight for each single hypergraph can make the constructed object hypergraph more representative. These weights can be learned via training samples, such as the labeled data from user relevance feedback or the training data in an object classification task. Given such training samples, a joint learning process can be conducted by learning both the relevance scores and the hypergraph weights simultaneously. In this scenario, the objective function can be rewritten as:

$$
\arg \min_{f, \alpha} \Phi (f, \alpha) = \arg \min_f \left\{ \lambda R_{\text{emp}}(f) + \Omega (f) + \mu \Xi \alpha \right\}, \tag{7.48}
$$

where $\Xi \alpha$ is a two-norm regularizer of the hypergraph weights.

The objective function can be further rewritten as

$$\min_{f,\alpha} \Phi(f,\alpha) = \min_{f,\alpha} \frac{1}{2} \sum_{i=1}^{n_g} \alpha_i \sum_{e \in E} \sum_{u,v \in V_i} \frac{w_i(e) h_i(u,e) h_i(v,e)}{\delta_i(e)} \left(\frac{f_u}{\sqrt{d_i(u)}} - \frac{f_v}{\sqrt{d_i(v)}} \right)^2$$

$$+ \mu \sum_{i=1}^{n_g} \alpha_i^2 + \lambda \|f - y\|^2$$

$$= \min_{f,\alpha} f^T \sum_{i=1}^{n_g} \alpha_i (\mathbf{I} - \Theta_i) f + \mu \sum_{i=1}^{n_g} \alpha_i^2 + \lambda \|f - y\|^2$$

$$\text{s.t.} \quad \sum_{i=1}^{n_g} \alpha_i = 1, \mu > 0, \lambda > 0. \tag{7.49}$$

Here, $\alpha = \left[\alpha_1, \alpha_2, \ldots, \alpha_{n_g} \right]^T$.

The above problem can be solved via alternating optimization. The hypergraph weights α can be first fixed and f is optimized. The task reduces to

$$\min_f f^T \sum_{i=1}^{n_g} \alpha_i (\mathbf{I} - \Theta_i) f + \lambda \|f - y\|^2$$

$$\text{s.t.} \quad \lambda > 0, \tag{7.50}$$

where $\Theta_i = \mathbf{D}_{vi}^{-(1/2)} \mathbf{H}_i \mathbf{W}_i \mathbf{D}_{ei}^{-1} \mathbf{H}_i^T \mathbf{D}_{vi}^{-(1/2)}$.

Let $\Delta = \sum_{i=1}^{n_g} \alpha_i (\mathbf{I} - \Theta_i) = \mathbf{I} - \sum_{i=1}^{n_g} \alpha_i \Theta_i = \mathbf{I} - \Theta$, where $\Theta = \sum_{i=1}^{n_g} \alpha_i \Theta_i$. It can be solved by

$$f = \left(\mathbf{I} + \frac{1}{\lambda} \Delta \right)^{-1} y. \tag{7.51}$$

Then, f is fixed and α can be optimized. The optimization task reduces to

$$\min_\alpha f^T \sum_{i=1}^{n_g} \alpha_i (\mathbf{I} - \Theta_i) f + \mu \sum_{i=1}^{n_g} \alpha_i^2$$

$$\text{s.t.} \quad \sum_{i=1}^{n_g} \alpha_i = 1, \mu > 0. \tag{7.52}$$

To solve this problem, the Lagrangian is used to rewrite the task as

$$\min_{\alpha,\eta} f^T \sum_{i=1}^{n_g} \alpha_i (\mathbf{I} - \Theta_i) f + \mu \sum_{i=1}^{n_g} \alpha_i^2 + \eta \left(\sum_{i=1}^{n_g} \alpha_i - 1 \right). \qquad (7.53)$$

This problem can be solved by

$$\eta = \frac{-f^T \sum_{i=1}^{n_g} (\mathbf{I} - \Theta_i) f - 2\mu}{n_g} \qquad (7.54)$$

and

$$\alpha_i = \frac{1}{n_g} + \frac{f^T \sum_{i=1}^{n_g} (\mathbf{I} - \Theta_i) f}{2 n_g \mu} - \frac{f^T (\mathbf{I} - \Theta_i) f}{2\mu}. \qquad (7.55)$$

In the above solution, each step can decrease the objective function $\Phi(f, \alpha)$, which has a lower bound of 0. Then, the convergence of the alternating optimization can be guaranteed. The learned optimal hypergraph weights can be used to achieve more accurate 3-D object modeling in the 3DOR.

7.3.5 Learning the Weights for Edges

In the last part the combined multiple hypergraphs are used to determine the weights for an optimal fused hypergraph structure. It is noted that the hypergraph-level combination can be regarded as a rough weighting; a fine weighting can be achieved by determining the edge-level weights, in which important edges can be assigned high weights and bad edges can be assigned low weights. All edges in one hypergraph must have the same weights in the hypergraph-level fusion, which is not the optimal solution for a well-designed object hypergraph.

Considering the optimal weighting learning for edges, the objective function can be written by

$$\arg \min_{f,w} \Phi(f, w) = \arg \min_{f} \left\{ \lambda R_{\text{emp}}(f) + \Omega(f) + \mu \sum w_i^2 \right\}, \qquad (7.56)$$

where $\sum w_i^2$ is a two-norm regularizer on the edge weights.

The objective function can be further rewritten as

$$\min_{f,w} \Phi(f, w) = \min_{f,w} \frac{1}{2} \sum_{e \in E_i u, v \in V} \frac{w_i(e) \, h_i(u, e) \, h_i(v, e)}{\delta_i(e)} \left(\frac{f_u}{\sqrt{d_i(u)}} - \frac{f_v}{\sqrt{d_i(v)}} \right)^2$$

$$+ \mu \sum_{i=1}^{n_2} w_i^2 + \lambda \|f - y\|^2$$

$$= \min_{f,w} f^T (\mathbf{I} - \Theta) f + \mu \sum_{i=1}^{n_e} w_i^2 + \lambda \|f - y\|^2$$

$$\text{s.t.} \quad \sum_{i=1}^{n_e} w_i = 1, \mu > 0, \lambda > 0. \tag{7.57}$$

Here, n_e is the number of edges in the object hypergraph. $\Theta = \mathbf{D}_v^{-(1/2)} \mathbf{H} \mathbf{W} \mathbf{D}_e^{-1} \mathbf{H}^T \mathbf{D}_v^{-(1/2)}$. Letting $\Delta = (\mathbf{I} - \Theta)$, the objective function can be solved by a similar alternating optimization. The edge weights w can first be fixed and f can be optimized. The task reduces to

$$\min_{f} f^T (\mathbf{I} - \Theta) f + \lambda \|f - y\|^2$$

$$\text{s.t.} \quad \lambda > 0. \tag{7.58}$$

The task can be solved according to

$$f = \left(\mathbf{I} + \frac{1}{\lambda} \Delta \right)^{-1} y. \tag{7.59}$$

Then, f is fixed and w can be optimized. The optimization task reduces to

$$\min_{w} f^T (\mathbf{I} - \Theta) f + \mu \sum_{l=1}^{n_e} w_i^2$$

$$\text{s.t.} \quad \sum_{i=1}^{n_e} w_i = 1, \mu > 0. \tag{7.60}$$

To solve this problem, the Lagrangian is employed to rewrite the task as

$$\min_{w,\eta} f^T (\mathbf{I} - \Theta) f + \mu \sum_{i=1}^{n_e} w_i^2 + \eta \left(\sum_{i=1}^{n_e} w_i - 1 \right)$$

$$= \min_{w,\eta} f^T \left(\mathbf{I} - \mathbf{D}_v^{-(1/2)} \mathbf{H} \mathbf{W} \mathbf{D}_e^{-1} \mathbf{H}^T \mathbf{D}_v^{-(1/2)} \right) f$$

$$+ \mu \sum_{i=1}^{n_e} w_i^2 + \eta \left(\sum_{i=1}^{n_e} w_i - 1 \right). \tag{7.61}$$

Letting $\Gamma = \mathbf{D}_v^{-(1/2)}\mathbf{H}$, the optimization problem above can be solved according to

$$\eta = \frac{f^T \Gamma f - 2\mu}{n_e} \qquad (7.62)$$

and

$$\omega_i = \frac{1}{n_e} - \frac{f^T \Gamma \mathbf{D}_e^{-1} \Gamma^T f}{2 n_e \mu} + \frac{f^T \Gamma_i D_e^{-1}(i,i)\, \Gamma_i^T f}{2\mu}, \qquad (7.63)$$

where Γ_i is the ith column of Γ.

These learned edge weights w can further improve the object hypergraph structure and make it more discriminative.

7.4 SUMMARY

In this chapter, we briefly reviewed learning-based 3DOR methods, including Hausdorff distance learning, bipartite graph learning, and hypergraph learning. In these methods, either the optimal distance metric or the underlying object relevance, or both, can be determined via the SSL process. In the Hausdorff distance learning method, the pairwise view distance metric can be optimally updated for the object-level distance. In the bipartite graph learning method, the object relevance is learned in a graph structure. The hypergraph formulation is also introduced in V3DOR, which can explore the high-order information among multiple views. To further improve the hypergraph structure, different extensions have been introduced in this chapter, including multiple hypergraph fusion, multiple hypergraph weight learning, and edge weight learning.

In comparison with previous methods, the learning-based methods can achieve relatively better 3DOR performance, which demonstrates the effectiveness of the learning-based technique in object matching and relevance estimation in experiments.

REFERENCES

[1] Chapelle O, Scholkopf B, Zien A. Semi-supervised learning, vol. 2. Cambridge: MIT Press; 2006.

[2] Zhou D, Bousquet O, Lal T, Weston J, Schokopf B. Learning with local and global consistency. In: Proceedings of NIPS; 2004.

[3] Seeger M. Learning with labeled and unlabeled data. Technical report, University of Edinburgh; 2001.

[4] Chapelle O, Schölkopf B, Zien A, et al. Semi-supervised learning, vol. 2. Cambridge, MA: MIT Press; 2006.

[5] Zhu X. Semi-supervised learning literature survey; 2005.

[6] Zhou D, Huang J, Schokopf B. Learning with hypergraphs: clustering, classification, and embedding. In: Proceedings of NIPS; 2007.

[7] Huang Y, Liu Q, Zhang S, Metaxas D. Image retrieval via probabilistic hypergraph ranking. In: Proceedings of IEEE Conference on Computer Vision and Pattern Recognition; 2010.

[8] Bu J, Tan S, Chen C, Wang C, Wu H, Zhang L, et al. Music recommendation by unified hypergraph: combining social media information and music content. In: Proceedings of MM; 2010.

[9] Gao Y, Wang M, Ji R, Wu X, Dai Q. 3D object retrieval with Hausdorff distance learning. IEEE Trans Ind Electron 2014;61(4):2088-98.

[10] Lu K, Ji R, Tang J, Gao Y. Learning-based bipartite graph matching for view-based 3D model retrieval. IEEE Trans Image Process 2014;23(10):4553-63.

[11] Gao Y, Wang M, Tao D, Ji R, Dai Q. 3D object retrieval and recognition with hypergraph analysis. IEEE Trans Image Process 2012;21(9):4290-303.

[12] Atallah MJ. A linear time algorithm for the Hausdorff distance between convex polygons. Inf Process Lett 1983;17:207-9.

[13] Dubuisson MP, Jain AK. Modified Hausdorff distance for object matching. In: Proceedings of the IAPR International Conference on Pattern Recognition; 1994. p. 566-8.

[14] Takeda H, Farsiu S, Milanfar P. Kernel regression for image processing and reconstruction. IEEE Trans Image Process 2007;16(2):349-66.

[15] Xing E, Ng A, Jordan M, Russell S. Distance metric learning with application to clustering with side-information. In: Advances in Neural Information Processing Systems; 2003.

[16] Zhang Z, Kwok J, Yeung D. Parametric distance metric learning with label information. In: International Joint Conference on Artificial Intelligence; 2003.

[17] Khotanzad A, Hong YH. Invariant image recognition by Zernike moments. IEEE Trans Pattern Anal Mach Intell 1990;12(5):489-97.

[18] Gao Y, Dai Q, Wang M, Zhang N. 3D model retrieval using weighted bipartite graph matching. In: Signal Process Image Commun 2011;26(1):39-47.

[19] Steinbach M, Karypis G, Kumar V. A comparison of document clustering techniques. In: Proceedings of KDD Workshop on TextMining; 2000.

[20] Chen H, Bhanu B. Efficient recognition of highly similar 3D objects in range images. IEEE Trans Pattern Anal Mach Intell 2009;31(1):172-9.

[21] Huang Y, Liu Q, Metaxas D. Video object segmentation by hypergraph cut. In: Proceedings of the IEEE Computer Society Conference on Computer Vision and Pattern Recognition; 2009. p. 1738-45.

[22] Xia S, Hancock E. Clustering using class specific hyper graphs. Lect Notes Comput Sci 2008;5342:318-28.

[23] Zass R, Shashua A. Probabilistic graph and hypergraph matching. In: Proceedings of the IEEE Computer Society Conference on Computer Vision and Pattern Recognition; 2008. p. 1-8.

[24] Gao Y, Wang M, Yan S, Shen J, Tao D. Tag-based social image search with visual-text joint hypergraph learning. In: Proceedings of Proceedings of ACM Conference on Multimedia; 2011. p. 1517-20.

[25] Gao Y, Wang M, Zha Z, Shen J, Li X, Wu X. Visual-textual joint relevance learning for tag-based social image search. IEEE Trans Image Process 2013;22(1):363-76.

[26] Xia S, Hancock E. 3D object recognition using hyper-graphs and ranked local invariant features. Lect Notes Comput Sci 2008;5342:117-26.

[27] Xia S, Hancock E. Learning large scale class specific hyper graphs for object recognition. In: Proceedings of the International Conference on Image and Graphics; 2008. p. 366-71.

[28] Wong AKC, Lu SW. Recognition and shape synthesis of 3D objects based on attributed hyper-graphs. IEEE Transactions on Pattern Analysis and Machine Intelligence 1989;11(3):279-90.

[29] Duda RO, Hart PE. Pattern classification and scene analysis. New York: Wiley; 1973.

PART IV

Conclusions and Future Work

CHAPTER 8

Conclusions and Future Work

8.1 SUMMARY OF THIS BOOK

V3DOR [1–3] has attracted extensive research efforts and has become an exciting new research field. In this book, we systematically introduce V3DOR, from basic ideas to current state-of-the-art methods. We also summarize our recent progress in this research area.

In the first part of this book, we explain the background of 3DOR. Then, we introduce a comparison between M3DOR and V3DOR. In this part, the basic ideas for V3DOR, primary challenges, and benchmarks are introduced. Although there are already many existing benchmarks, large-scale 3-D object data sets, particularly those with depth data, are still required for further study.

In the second part, we introduce state-of-the-art methods in view extraction, selection, and representation. View extraction is the fundamental process for V3DOR and a set of complete but compact views can significantly aid 3-D object representation. To this end, we introduce our spatial-structure circular descriptor (SSCD) [4]. There are two objectives of view selection: reducing the redundancy in multiple views and obtaining discriminatory views; most existing view selections focus on the first objective. We furthermore introduce our interactive view selection method [5], which can incrementally select discriminatory views with the help of interactions from the user. View representation consists of two parts: view feature extraction and view weighting. We introduce the bag-of-region-words (BoRW) descriptor [6] and the weight learning methods for multiple views [7] in this part. We note that existing view features still have limitations, such as a reduced ability to describe partial objects and the cross-view information.

In the third part, we introduce the view-based 3-D object comparison methods. In Chapter 6, the object-matching methods are provided. Generally, multiple view-based object matching [8, 9] can be regarded as a many-to-many matching task. We introduce some fundamental distance metrics and our methods, including a bipartite graph matching method [10] and a probabilistic matching method [11], to calculate the distance between two 3-D objects. These methods are based on the direct pairwise view distance. We furthermore introduce a Gaussian mixture model (GMM) formulation-based method [12], which can predict the view distribution instead of the exact views.

In Chapter 7, we introduce our learning-based methods, which extend beyond traditional pairwise object-matching approaches. On the one hand, we propose to determine optimal distance metrics, such as Hausdorff distance [13] and bipartite graph matching [14]. On the other hand, we also propose to determine the underlying relationship among 3-D objects, using either a simple graph framework (with the bipartite graph matching distance measure) or the hypergraph framework [15]. The merit of our learning-based V3DOR methods mainly lies in their ability to elucidate the structure behind both the labeled and unlabeled data, which can achieve better 3DOR performance.

8.2 FUTURE WORK

Although significant progress [1, 16, 17] has been made with V3DOR, there are still many open problems that require further investigation, for example, the big data issues, feature extraction, multiple-view matching, multimodal data problems, and geographical location-based applications.

8.2.1 The Issue of Big Data

Nowadays, we all face the issue of large data sets. The volume of 3-D object data is increasing rapidly on the Internet. The development of 3-D technologies has led to widespread applications, such as 3-D printers. This large quantity of 3-D object data further generates new challenges in V3DOR. A positive aspect is that these large data sets can provide much more 3-D information than ever before. However, a negative aspect of the data sets arises from challenges of data storage and processing. Future research will be devoted to addressing the big 3-D data, building efficient indices, extracting effective features, and determining semantics from large data sets.

8.2.2 Feature Extraction

The existing view features for 3-D objects still suffer from a limited descriptive ability with regard to partial information and cross-view correlation.

With rapidly developing techniques aimed at in-depth studies, new feature learning methods may be produced to handle even larger data sets.

8.2.3 Multiple-View Matching

Although there are many existing multiple-view matching algorithms for 3DOR, it is still a challenging task to determine the semantic relevance among 3-D objects using multiple views. Several methods use a probabilistic method to formulate the relationship among 3-D objects. Because each 3-D object is described by a group of views, the relationships among 3-D objects are more complex than the relationships between just two images. Thoroughly investigating the cross-view correlations clearly requires further investigation.

8.2.4 Multimodal Data

Multimedia analysis has created a revolution from text-based, content-based studies to social media analyses today. The devices that generate data are diverse because of the range of applications that exist. Presently, mobile devices with cameras, such as iPads, Google phones, iPhones, and other handheld mobile devices, can capture large-scale images every minute and everywhere. Billions of photos on Flickr, Facebook, and Foursquare have been uploaded by individual users. More sensors are providing diverse data from different applications, including surveillance systems and remote imaging systems. These diverse data lead to a multimodal property from two perspectives. From the perspective of the data style, multiple modalities are involved, including traditional local 3-D objects, multiple views, range images, depth images, and other novel modalities for 3-D information descriptions. These multiple modalities have been seen from the very beginning of data collection to the end of search function design. From the perspective of data resources, 3-D data exist not only in local data centers but also in many other platforms, such as the 3-D objects on the Internet, multiple-view data from websites (e.g., Amazon and eBay), and depth data generated by Kinect in daily life. This multimodal information provides rich data for 3-D object analysis, along with the associated challenges of data processing across different media and platforms.

8.2.5 Geographical Location-Based Applications

The multiple views have significant potential in geolocation-based applications. Mobile/location-based search has attracted attention in recent years. In a specific geographical region, there can be different data generated by individual users (phone cameras) and surveillance systems, together with other data from the Internet with geographical location tags, such as tweets, posters, and check-ins in Foursquare. All these data provide new opportunities for the next stage of mobile search. Intelligent city has been another hot topic in recent years. Multiple-view analysis has shown its superiority in intelligent city computing, such as tracking, model reconstruction, recognition, and virtual city navigation. Other applications may include location-based recommendations, online social media analysis, and so on. All these applications can benefit from view-based object retrieval and related analysis, which can provide rich information from multimodal data resources. Multimodal and multiresource data are the main challenges to these applications for view-based object retrieval.

REFERENCES

[1] Bimbo AD, Pala PS. Content-based retrieval of 3D models. ACM Trans Multimed Comput Commun Appl 2007;2(1):20-43.

[2] Chen DY, Tian XP, Shen YT, Ouhyoung M. On visual similarity based 3D model retrieval. Comput Graph Forum 2003;22(3):223-32.

[3] Ohbuchi R, Osada K, Furuya T, Banno T. Salient local visual features for shape based 3D model retrieval. In: Proceedings of IEEE Conference on Shape Modeling and Applications; 2008. p. 93-102.

[4] Gao Y, Dai QH, Zhang NY. 3D model comparison using spatial structure circular descriptor. Pattern Recogn 2010;43(3):1142-51.

[5] Gao Y, Wang M, Zha Z, Tian Q, Dai Q, Zhang N. Less is more: efficient 3D object retrieval with query view selection. IEEE Trans Multimed 2011;11(5):1007-18.

[6] Gao Y, Yang Y, Dai Q, Zhang N. 3D object retrieval with bag-of-region-words. ACM Conf Multimed; 2010. p. 955-8.

[7] Gao Y, Wang M, Ji R, Zha Z, Shen J. K-partite graph reinforcement and its application in multimedia information retrieval. In: Inf Sci 2012;194:224-39.

[8] Atallah MJ. A linear time algorithm for the Hausdorff distance between convex polygons. Inf Process Lett 1983;17:207-9.

[9] Dubuisson MP, Jain AK. Modified Hausdorff distance for object matching. In: Proceedings of the IAPR International Conference on Pattern Recognition; 1994. p. 566-8.

[10] Gao Y, Dai Q, Wang M, Zhang N. 3D model retrieval using weighted bipartite graph matching. Signal Process Image Commun 2011;26(1):39-47.

[11] Gao Y, Tang J, Hong R, Yan S, Dai Q, Zhang N, et al. Camera constraint-free view-based 3D object retrieval. IEEE Trans Image Process 2012;21(4):2269-81.

[12] Wang M, Gao Y, Lu K, Rui Y. View-based discriminative probabilistic modeling for 3D object retrieval and recognition. IEEE Trans Image Process 2013;22(4):1395-407.

[13] Gao Y, Wang M, Ji R, Wu X, Dai Q. 3D object retrieval with Hausdorff distance learning. IEEE Trans Ind Electron 2014;61(4):2088-98.

[14] Lu K, Ji R, Tang J, Gao Y. Learning-based bipartite graph matching for view-based 3D model retrieval. IEEE Trans Image Process 2014;23(10):4553-63.

[15] Gao Y, Wang M, Tao D, Ji R, Dai Q. 3D object retrieval and recognition with hypergraph analysis. IEEE Trans Image Process 2012;21(9):4290-303.

[16] Tangelder JWH, Veltkamp RC. A survey of content based 3D shape retrieval methods. Multimed Tools Appl 2008;39:441-71.

[17] Yang Y, Lin H, Zhang Y. Content-based 3-D model retrieval: a survey. IEEE Trans Syst Man Cybern Part C Appl Rev 2007;37:1081-98.

Printed by Printforce, the Netherlands